Becoming Who GOD Wants You to Be

60 Meditations for Personal Spiritual Direction

W. Paul Jones

UPPER ROOM BOOKS®
NASHVILLE

To the Trappist Lay Associates of Assumption Abbey
(Ava, Missouri)

*Our work together
in applying the disciplines of Christian spirituality
to daily life has inspired me to believe in
the value of self-guided spiritual direction.*

CONTENTS

CONTENTS

CONTENTS

Self-Guidance

An Introduction

Spiritual Direction

WHAT IS IT?

THE PURPOSE OF THIS BOOK is to provide guidance for the person who wishes to grow spiritually but may not have a personal spiritual director as a companion on his or her pilgrimage. For a number of years, I have provided spiritual direction for a wide array of persons using various working arrangements such as face-to-face, telephone, and e-mail. The direct option is preferable, yet for many persons this type of spiritual guidance is unavailable. Consequently, this book is a tool for facilitating spiritual direction in the form of self-guidance.

The title *spiritual director* can be misleading, so I should state first that the only authentic director is the Holy Spirit. The task of spiritual direction, therefore, is to discern the direction and implications of the Spirit's leadings. The term *spiritual director* only recently came to the attention of the contemporary church, but its equivalency is also operative in secular arenas. You might hear the terms *coach* or *trainer*—someone who has sufficient expertise to be contracted for helping others attain growth in a particular area, from physical stamina to yoga. In the professional world, *mentors* use their own knowledge and experience to help form others in their pursuit of related goals. What we are seeing is something of a return to the idea of apprenticeship, a method used in the past as a way to learn and practice a trade. Individuals are not the only ones seeking this type of guidance; companies, agencies, and corporations are hiring consultants to help create mission statements that clarify and then oversee a faithful attainment of an effective and efficient working environment.

Spiritual direction, under various names, has always been an important practice in the church. Since it is impossible to become a Christian and live out a Christian life alone, spiritual direction is useful and downright necessary. Jesus served as spiritual director for his select twelve, forming them through the slow process of faithful discipleship. His direction was one of presence and teaching. The disciples' time spent in formation with Jesus prepared them to be spiritual directors for the fledgling Christian communities that formed after the resurrection. Paul provided spiritual direction by letter, coupled with occasional personal visits. The early desert mothers and fathers were persons whose holiness was such that others came to their huts and asked, "Please, a word for my soul." Monasteries were established around such holy persons to provide communal spiritual direction, with monks held accountable under the counsel of an abbot or abbess as spiritual guide.

Jesus' favorite name for the calling of spiritual director was *shepherd*, a term that the prophets had used for their own vocation with Israel. An equivalent term today is *pastor* when referring to clergy—meaning that the tasks of preaching, teaching, organizing, and administering the sacraments are intended to be ways of pasturing the sheep into abundant lives. Jesus said, "I am the good shepherd. I know my own and my own know me" (John 10:14).

With Jesus as our model, we should perhaps be a bit wary of the term *director*. Jesus' preferred method of formation was less instructional and more relational in telling of parables that evoked self-guidance. He carefully chose his stories as exercises through which his followers might recognize the Spirit's workings in their everyday lives. Jesus spoke of lost items, belligerent teenagers, sowing seeds, caring for animals, births, disappointments, calamities, healings, and death—intersecting the scope of the human condition with a richness of themes. He would conclude by asking open-ended questions, such as, "Which of these three, do you think, was a neighbor to the man who fell into the hands of the robbers?" (Luke 10:36) or "Which of the two did the will of his father?" (Matt. 21:31). Jesus encouraged self-guidance through exercises in self-discernment. That is what this book is about.

Saint Paul was the master of providing epistolary spiritual direction. His letters proved to be so helpful, even for those to whom they were not addressed, that they were collected as meditations for spiritual direction. Thus, the first New Testament writings are collections of spiritual direction letters. Some of his letters provided love and prayerful encouragement; others focused on instruction; and still others were direct engagements with persons he felt were going astray. Paul would conclude his letters with a charge to his readers: "Finally, brothers and sisters, farewell. Put things in order, listen to my appeal, agree with one another, live in peace" (2 Cor. 13:11).

The radicalness of the gospel gradually dissipates when the vehicles for accountable spiritual direction become domesticated in the lifestyle of secular culture. Yet, when new forms of spiritual direction emerge, the church can undergo effective renewal. While prophetic voices are necessary for us to maintain faithfulness, the church seems better able to hear nondefensively the transforming power of the gospel when joys and sorrows can be shared so that the disciplining truth can be spoken and heard. Supportive accountability—whether individual or corporate—is what spiritual direction is about.

A good example of such spiritual direction is the Wesleyan effort at renewing Anglicanism, which birthed Methodism and other related groups. Wesley insisted that none of his ministers should preach anywhere unless each showed that there would be provisions for spiritual direction in the congregations. Otherwise, the preacher would be inviting persons into a new way of living without providing the means for doing so. Since one-on-one direction was impractical, Wesley developed various types of communal spiritual direction that fostered Christian growth. Members of the church could share their lives with one another so that each person became willing to be asked point-blank, "How are you really?" *Fine* was an unacceptable answer. This bonding through loving accountability encouraged life's basic questions to surface: Who am I?; Where did I come from?; Where am I going?; What am I on this earth?; What do I need to change?; and What am I to do with my life? No vital dimensions of living were neglected—relationships, finances, disciplines, habits, prayer, dispositions, worship, temptations, sins. Corporate spiritual direction provides a loving discipline whereby we see social holiness as responsible wholeness. *Sanctification* is the theological name for the ongoing process of growing in grace. Through sanctification, you could say that we are never Christians but always becoming so. The 2012 General Conference of The United Methodist Church took a beginning step in restoring this tradition by insisting that all pastors and deacons have and use a spiritual guide, pastoral counselor, or vocational mentor.

Unfortunately, the contemporary church has steadily lost not only its traditional instruments for spiritual direction but even the idea of what it is and thus its indispensability. Not surprisingly, Alcoholics Anonymous and various other 12-step programs that spun off from this type of spiritual direction have been filling this void—offering what is actually a distillation of the dynamic that characterizes Christian spiritual direction. Mushrooming from its originating concern for alcoholics, AA's method is effectively applied to numerous addictions and issues, from drugs to obesity. AA's process begins when, after acknowledging our need, we enter a group that can provide supportive accountability sufficient for us to make a clean inventory of our living, ready for an ongoing method of confession that will reach into the hidden nooks and shadowy crannies of our lives. Confession is followed by the powerful act of forgiveness, washing clean our pasts. Once gifted with the freshness of a new beginning, we are able to make amends with those we have hurt, reoriented through commitment to a new future. With the help of a personal sponsor throughout, the 12-step process is lifelong, rooted in the awareness that without ongoing accountability recidivism is likely, if not inevitable. Wherever 12-step meetings are held and for whatever reason, the liturgy, so to speak, is the same, reflecting the power of repetition.

Spiritual direction need not focus on one specific problem. Christianity is rooted in the premise that all humans are fallen, meaning there is a chasm between who we are and who we are intended to be. None of us is perfect or even close. One way or another, each of us is bruised, scarred, wounded, hurt, insecure, resentful, angry, self-doubting, or restless. As a result, we are tempted to hide who we really are, perhaps even from ourselves. Life's basic temptations, even for Jesus, are possessions, prestige, and power. While secular society promises these as rewards for our conformity to its values, Christianity recognizes them as self-defeating temptations that cloak what Thoreau called our "quiet desperation," that is, existing without living, intent on quantity without quality, experiencing feelings without depth, amused by what is without meaning. Gandhi's words on the seven deadly sins are, "Pleasure without conscience, knowledge without character, wealth without work, commerce without morality, science without humanity, worship without sacrifice, and politics without principle." Trying to overcome such temptations on our own can feel like the self who is unable to hold accountable the self who is resisting change. Somehow we must be awakened to understand that our lives' task is to become the best version of our selves that we were created to be.

Salvation, meaning "to be rendered healthy and whole," is the theological term for this journey of awakening. We cannot take this journey alone because we were created to love by being loved by others, specifically and originally by God. Consequently, this is possible only when we become willing to be held accountable for loving as we are being loved by God. We know we need spiritual direction when we are awakened by life's roughness into recognizing the difference between existing and living. Saint Paul describes this awareness well: "I do not understand my own actions. For I do not do what I want, but I do the very thing I hate. . . . Who will rescue me . . . ?" (Rom. 7:15, 24). The answer he received on the Damascus road was to enter the city and wait, which he did for three days and three nights in a house on Straight Street, and a spiritual director named Ananias came to him there (see Acts 9:10-19).

The prophets served as the spiritual directors for Israel in general and Israel's leaders in particular. One particular session between the prophet Nathan and King David helps us sense the prophetic edge of spiritual direction. Nathan tells David the story of a wealthy man who owns many sheep, yet he kills for his own feasting the only lamb belonging to a poor man. David erupted, "The man who has done this deserves to die" (2 Sam. 12:5). "You are the man!" Nathan responded (12:7). Tough love means holding a mirror up to the face of a person we love. In Jesus, we see our own reflection, yet we, unlike King David, are often tempted to destroy the mirror rather than accept the reflection.

itual direction comes in varied forms. It can happen with a close
friend if the relationship is grounded in mutual honesty. A journal can
aid personal spiritual direction if it is used as a candid mirror. But best of
all is to have a spiritual director who personally models spiritual growth,
has a talent for wise discernment, and has a loving disposition sufficient
to provide supportive accountability and companionship. Such directors are given various titles—guru, soul friend, coach, guide, resource,
confessor, companion, saint, or midwife. But since each of these might
suggest a different approach to direction, I prefer seeing these names
not as alternative types but as diverse functions that a talented spiritual
director might use at different times, depending on the particular issue or
situation. Put most succinctly, spiritual directors are those who know us
so well that they can sing our song when we forget the words, reminding
us of our plot when we get lost in the thicket of its details.

I continue to use the title *spiritual director* because of its rich history,
but we must not be misled. On the one hand, the word *director* should
not suggest someone who is unduly directive. On the other hand, the
word *spiritual* should not focus us on only the religious dimension of
our lives. *Spiritual* refers to one's total lifestyle as this emerges from one's
basic life-orientation. Each of us has such a center—where our physical,
moral, intellectual, volitional, and emotional dimensions intersect and
interpenetrate at a depth deserving the name *soul*.

Know Your Spiritual Director

WHO AM I? WHO ARE YOU?

An initial face-to-face spiritual direction session should be spent in sufficient mutual sharing to give both director and directee the sense of a good fit. For such rapport, we must be assured that our directors will not be inclined to impose their own issues, biases, and hang-ups on us but content instead to be guides in identifying the Spirit's hinting, nudging, and luring. Directors cannot be totally objective, so we should be aware of their particular subjectivities. For this, we need to hear enough of their stories to be able to neutralize any unhelpful biases and to sense their vulnerabilities sufficiently to be able to trust that they will be caring when our flaws are uncovered. Trust deepens when we sense through the director that our seemingly overgrown and lonely paths are within hailing distance of a fellow traveling companion.

So who am I really—the one who is offering to be your spiritual director by using this book for self-guidance? I am as unique as I suspect you are. Coal dust resides in my lungs, as I was born in Appalachia, the only child of a mining family. Early on, I sensed in my father's daily farewells the possibility of premature endings. My birth was a painful life-and-death struggle between my mother and me—one that would continue in various ways until her self-imposed death. Life back then centered around the cemetery on the hill—dates, walks, picnics, funerals. My introverted parents attempted to inhibit my extroverted temperament, which encouraged me to live in an alternative poetic world of my own making. It became natural for me to perceive situations and persons not so much for what they were as for what they could be. My values were shaped by the Great Depression, and I learned to scavenge among trash for hidden potential. Creating gave me joy, whether I was building villages from sand piles or forts from discarded crates. The enforced silence of my introverted parents, accompanied by their conservative literal piety, discouraged me from considering myself spiritual. The closest I came to feeling spiritual was when I stood at the mouth of a mine shaft that disappeared for miles into the earth's mystery. Or when I admired the stained-glass windows in church. But the most spiritual places for me were usually connected with trees, high rocks, and water. My thin body and wire-rimmed glasses were a bit of a trial, and I felt shamed by comic-book superheroes ridiculing bespectacled ninety-pound weaklings.

I was reared on a diet of conditional love, with tickets for acceptance needing to be earned only after accomplishing whatever was expected extremely well and quickly. My father's schooling ended with the third grade, so college seemed unattainable until a late scholarship from a junior college provided me with an exit from the steel mills.

Looking back now, it seems that I never made an important decision in my life, not really. Doors opened, and it made no sense not to walk through them. Surely my first word as a child was *Why*, so the path into philosophy and theology was natural. In graduate school at Yale, I learned that I had a brain, and after attaining three degrees a teaching position at Princeton was offered. When teaching about religion began to feel passive, I was invited to help create a new seminary. Walking in, I was drawn into developing an action-reflection methodology, which is a way of learning by reflective doing. I never looked back.

These were the 1960s, and the radicalness of the gospel and the Woodstock dream began commingling in my mind. The next two decades were something of a rapid-fire blur. I visited Cuba and was captivated by the contrast between a socialist society committed to mutual responsibility and my country rooted in competitive individualism. I saw how my country's aggressive foreign policy looked from the inside of Nicaragua. I participated in the Moratorium March against the Vietnam War. My wife, five daughters, and I moved from suburbia into an inner-city tenement to form a Christian commune committed to social justice ministry.

I was a flower child at heart, believing that if white folks were awakened to see how they were hurting black folks, they would change. Instead my own awakening began when the National Guard killed students at Kent State and continued with the tragedy at Altamont, California. A concert of reconciliation was to be held there between the violence-prone Hell's Angels and the flower children to establish what they called another way. "Another way" was not reached, and a man was killed directly in front of the stage.

While I continued to be claimed by a vision of the kingdom of God against the backdrop of Woodstock, from that point on Altamont would be my lens. I began seeing how the human dilemma centers not in ignorance but in sin, with a deep darkness in each of us and in our society. I began seeing that what was needed was not a new ethic but new persons, entailing nothing less than a conversion of one's very disposition. All this happened at the same time that I was becoming burned out by my ministry. In social justice work, one is fortunate to gain one victory for every ten defeats. And any justice attained today will deteriorate into tomorrow's injustice. I had become a relentlessly driven man, whose life was interspersed with lectures, speeches, articles, and books to be written. I was unable to stop—or go on.

Again a door opened—and I stumbled into a monastery, a place I had thought to be as extinct as the dinosaurs. There I discovered a world of being instead of doing. Time was doled out one day at a time to be drunk to the dregs, and each evening the cup was handed back to be refilled. Loving acceptance was not earned but gift-wrapped. There was no private property, so by holding all things in common there was enough for everyone without need for possessiveness or competition. The echoing silence of the monastery forced me to sift through the ashes and scars of my past.

The path out of my quagmire felt like Frost's "Road Not Taken," but it wasn't. It turned out that many before me had taken it, and they called it the gospel. Saint Paul was the one who gave me the compass. To this day, his key passage is taped to my computer and my bathroom mirror, and I rehearse it daily lest I forget. Paul tells us that nothing in all creation "will be able to separate us from the love of God in Christ Jesus our Lord" (Rom. 8:39). To be loved—unconditionally, undeservedly, graciously, and always—not because of who I am but in spite of what I have done, is all I ever desired. Such a love is more than enough, and it gives new eyes through which to see the world. This love calls me to stand with God in Christ and thus with the poor and the rejected.

Later, I found myself at the threshold of a new experience, a new door, but it was a steel prison door, and it wouldn't open. As I relate in my book *A Different Kind of Cell*, I inexplicably found myself the spiritual director for the deadliest prisoner the federal prison system had ever known. Utterly uncontrollable, killing with his own hands five different persons at five different times, he was housed in a specially constructed steel and concrete vault outside the criminally insane wing of the U.S. Medical Center in Springfield, Missouri. Our relationship began by mail, but we later communicated by phone, and finally through a slot in his steel door. He was gradually transformed into one of the most caring persons I have ever known. Near the day that my monastery accepted him as a monk in absentia, he said, "Paul, if I can be forgiven, then no one is beyond the mercy of God." Since forming this relationship, abolishing the death penalty has become my passion.

So here I am now, having taken early retirement to be the Resident Director of the Hermitage Spiritual Retreat Center on Lake Pomme de Terre in the Ozark hills of southern Missouri. I give thanks for how the strands of my life have woven themselves into a tapestry whose theme is Eucharist. I celebrate this sacrament daily at my hermitage. Either alone or with others, I break the bread of the world's suffering, pour out the blood of Christ's love, and toast God's resurrection promise by lifting the joys and sorrows of all creation. At my simple altar, I kneel and offer thanksgiving for the transforming power of forgiveness offered through God's unconditional love in Christ and for the vision of the new heaven and earth where ox and lion shall eat together and God will wipe away all tears, for death shall be no more. Faith means wagering on these promises by living as if they are already so.

What does such living look like? It means having no unforgiven regrets, loving as if you have never been hurt, working in thankfulness for the gift of being cocreators with God, believing that you are where you are meant to be, treating others as the friend you wished you had, aging gracefully and faithfully, and being readied to die so that there is nothing left for death to take. So here I am, on a path that brought me to ordination as a United Methodist minister, then as a Roman Catholic priest, and now as a vowed Trappist Family Brother—all the while writing, praying, doing spiritual direction, and working for social justice. I can contentedly say with the psalmist that the lot marked out for me is my delight.

For those of you who care about such things, my Myers-Briggs temperament is ENTJ (Extroversion, Intuition, Thinking, Judging); and I am a Three in the Enneagram (Achiever), with wings Two (Helper) and Four (Individualist). While all of this might sound a bit heavy, I live my life much the way Jesus proposed: "Whoever does not receive the kingdom of God as a little child will never enter it" (Luke 18:17). I have tried to grow up, and many seem to take me seriously as if I have, but inside I have always been a child at heart, with Mickey Mouse as my patron saint. Now, who are you?

Using This Book

HERE'S HOW

THOUGH IDEAL, FACE-TO-FACE spiritual direction it is not always available or possible. Therefore, I have written this handbook as a functional substitute. The rest of the book is composed of short meditations distilling basic themes that have emerged from spiritual direction sessions over the years. They are arranged alphabetically by topic, but the order is otherwise arbitrary.

I invite you to let me function as your spiritual director through these meditations. With a notebook and pen or pencil, find a private space to spend half an hour. Choose a meditation whose title seems engaging, or choose one at random. Get comfortable, take several deep breaths, pray to be open and centered as to let go of distractions. Then slowly read the meditation, recording any ongoing responses. Take your time so that the exercise becomes a dialogue, letting thoughts, ideas, and images touch your present situation. You may prefer to underline and write in the margins of the book, saving the notebook for summary comments. Rereading the meditation is often helpful. When finished, read over your comments and do two things: underline thoughts that are worth remembering, or at least revisiting; and make yourself an assignment as to how you can apply some insight, addition, or correction to your daily life. After I work with persons in discerning their assignments, we always decide how they will be held accountable, perhaps by telephone or e-mail. In self-guided spiritual direction, a marked calendar is useful.

Hopefully some of these meditations will be directly relevant to your life. Others may suggest new ideas and activities worth exploring. Still others may evoke resistance or considerable disagreement, making it worth asking questions and answering with your own understanding.

Spiritual directors should never be regarded as experts who are beyond questioning. Use us only as a means of helping you do what alone is important—to be mindfully engaged in discerning what the Spirit is doing on your pilgrimage.

Meditations for Self-Guidance

Abandonment

THE POWER OF PROMISE

Through my work in spiritual direction, I find that many people have a fear of abandonment. As an only child, I felt that fear especially when my parents would go out for an evening. I didn't know if I could trust the promise that my parents would return because of the lurking fear that one night they wouldn't—and I'd be alone always.

Understandably, I find comfort in Jesus' promise of promises: "I will not leave you desolate; I will come to you" (John 14:18, RSV). In seminary I knew who my favorite theologian would be the day my professor said that Karl Barth's God was the one who made and kept promises. My favorite place as a boy was climbing to the highest branch of the cherry tree in our yard. From there you could almost see China—or at least the far edge of the alley. In that tree I would dream that someday a tree house might reside there. One Sunday the minister shared Jesus' promise to "prepare a place for you" (John 14:3). I knew a better translation: "I go to build a tree house for you."

This image has remained throughout the years, and I encountered another scripture passage that completed the childhood portrait. I would move in, and there would be a knock on my tree house door. There he would be as promised. He would say, "I will come in to you and eat with you, and you with me" (Rev. 3:20). Even today while receiving Communion, this image of playing house together returns. It's all about being able to trust promises.

➤ **Is abandonment a primary fear hiding inside you or are you haunted by a different fear?**

Accountability

A TEST

I wonder if you are like me and find the Holy Spirit to be a vague something or other, wavering somewhere between an it and an abstract who. I find Saint Paul helpful in making the Spirit tangible by shifting focus from a what to a therefore, from a something to a consequence. He suggests recognizing the Holy Spirit in terms of gifts. While at first glance the Spirit's nine fruits may seem vague, I find them painfully concrete when used as an index in spiritual direction. In self-grading, I assign a number between one and ten, with ten being highest. Let me illustrate how this works by scoring myself according to Saint Paul's identification of the Spirit's fruits:

- *Love.* I do fairly well here, at least with family and friends. I confess being a bit shaky with the turn-the-other-cheek bit when someone seems to hurt me intentionally. As for the "just as you did it to one of the least of these" (Matt. 25:40) part, I'm really trying. Maybe that averages out as an eight.
- *Joy.* I'm playful, have a sense of humor, am fun to be around, and love life. I would give myself a nine.
- *Peace.* The best barometer here is the degree to which I experience God's presence as a deep, abiding sense of centering peace. At times this is a five—maybe lower when I become obsessed with attempting to prove myself. I find that I fluctuate uneasily between a three and a seven.
- *Patience.* I don't always have patience for others, especially in waiting for something to be done that I could do myself! I give myself a five.

- *Kindness.* I'm a compassionate sort, sensitive with a ready smile. I give myself a nine.
- *Goodness.* This is a tough one. My intentions tend to be better than my performance. Perhaps I would need help from others to decide.
- *Faithfulness.* I give myself an eight on most days.
- *Gentleness.* I'm a bit rambunctious and restless. How about an eight-and-a-half?
- *Self-control.* If this means highly disciplined, I'm maybe a six.

Now, how is the Spirit doing with you? Self-scoring involves some guesswork, so that is one reason why the church insists that one cannot be a Christian alone, for we are baptized into the body of Christ, and we all serve as members of the body. It is in seeing ourselves through the honest eyes of others that the score is more likely to be trustworthy, exposing those of us who are easy self-graders and those who are unduly self-deprecating. Wesley suggested that the serious Christian participate in a small group capable of providing such feedback within a loving context. Sanctification is the theological name for this process of "growth in grace," in which one either grows in the gifts of the Spirit or deteriorates into tasteless salt.

It is helpful, then, to use Saint Paul's diagnostic instrument both in solitary and in communal contexts. By charting your spiritual blood pressure over a period of time, you can detect tendencies needing to be starved to death through neglect, those needing direct attack, and those best relinquished totally to the Spirit for guidance. But be careful, for after the Spirit reconstructs your foundation, you will likely be facing a complete overhaul.

- **Share your scoring with a friend and ask for an honest response. Would it help if the two of you held each other accountable by doing periodic self-testing?**

Alone

IN A PLACE APART

I suspect that in growing up many of us had a special place that we might now be tempted to call sacred. Actually, I had two such spaces. One was my hiding place under the back porch where I could go to cry privately. The second was a cherry tree in the backyard, whose top branches I used for dreaming. This may account for why I have long been taken by a particular story about the prophet Elisha (see 2 Kings 4:8-10). A wealthy couple were delighted that Elisha liked to stop by their home when he was traveling nearby. So they built him a little room on the roof. Simply furnished, it contained only a bed, table, chair, and lamp. This was where Elisha would come and find spiritual renewal.

Each of us needs such a place—wriggling under a back porch, climbing a special tree, or shutting the door to make a room private. Our society obsesses over constant activity and noisy gadgets, which drain us in a way that only sacred space can fill. Jesus insisted on taking time apart, modeling this for his disciples. He found solace in the sacred, solitary hills. "In the morning, while it was still very dark, [Jesus] got up and went out to a deserted place, and there he prayed" (Mark 1:35). Even during his final days in Jerusalem, "[Jesus] went, as was his custom, to the Mount of Olives" (Luke 22:39).

Vacations are supposed to be yearly sabbaticals for guaranteeing such sacred time and space for restoration. Yet the drive of our culture so molds us that we squander even these opportunities with frantic doings—traveling five thousand miles in a week to see it all, returning more exhausted than when we left. Ironically, even if we would respect this yearning for time apart, in all likelihood we would be gridlocked by an inability to know what to do. Thus the straightforward proposal by our desert parents is more urgent now than ever. They insisted, "Go into your cell, and it will teach you everything." Each of us needs a borrowed equivalent of Elisha's little room. Behind the closed door is where we can relearn with the Spirit's help the peaceful playfulness of solitude that we knew as a child but have forgotten.

→ **Do you have a sacred space, or do you need to find one? How could you make it more sacred? Ideally, how often would you visit your sacred space?**

Asceticism

AS A MEANS

Early in my childhood, I was made to feel that the seriousness of being a Christian was to be measured by how much I forfeited, denied myself, and gave up. The austere Carthusian Order, founded by Saint Bruno (1035–1101), is legendary for what is sometimes called a world-denying asceticism. Rigorous living was not uncommon in the landscape of Christian history, but if this is seen as bleakness endured to earn eternal life, there is good reason to question if it is Christian. Christianity regards this earth as a jewel of God's creativity, viewing history as the theater for divine glory. Certainly we need some separation between Christian communal living and modern society's competitive individualism, but would it not be more faithful for Christians to work with this world rather than against it? Wouldn't a Christ-transforming culture be more Christian than a Christ-denying culture?

While there have been times when Christianity has taken on a world-disdaining aura, a corrective comes in realizing how often the lifestyle of even our most acclaimed ascetics and mystics is not rooted in an otherworldly preoccupation. In Bruno we find a person whose early life was highly successful in terms of wealth, education, and position. Then, as with many of us, there came a point when he became burned out by the hectic self-serving urban life of Reims and Rome. As an alternative, he was claimed by the majestically solemn mountains of France and, later, Italy. Surrounded by such beauty, as one biographer put it, his blood came alive. From the beginning of his experiment in solitude, Bruno's spirituality thrived on the poetic beauty of whatever environment God gifted him. One interpreter claimed that in the language of Bruno's writings we can feel the sun, smell the flowers, and be caressed by the breezes. Bruno marveled over the revolving seasons, the lulling sounds of running streams, and the beguilement of full moons. *Delight* was one of his favorite words.

Bruno's motto might sound harsh: "While the world changes, the cross stands firm." But for him, the cross guarantees the thoroughness of God's incarnation and immersion in all of creation. Thus he forged for his monks a sensuous lifestyle whereby to live as Christ's brides. He used the analogy of being Rachels and Marys and even suggested as analogy the Shunammite maiden who served as David's bedmate.

This same graceful charm of the Carthusians is evident in classic mystics such as Teresa of Avila, reformer of the equally strict Carmelite Order. Playing her flute to the delight of her community, she insisted that they dance together. Spiritually indispensable for her were frequent hikes with her novices into the majesty of the surrounding Spanish mountains. Likewise, John of the Cross, legendary for his spirituality of the "dark night of the soul," expressed Christian life in erotic poetry capable of making the unsuspecting reader blush.

Therefore, let these ascetic models underscore whatever path our Christian lives might take. The "world-denying" dimension of Christianity helps us reject whatever tempts, distracts, or diverts us from living as stewards of creation. Christ honored the world by making it his cherished home away from home. I like to believe that his tears on the cross were those of sadness in leaving a place he had come to love so dearly. In being grasped by creation's beauty, there arises in us the ache for resurrection.

true joy

⇢ **What are the world-denying aspects of your faith? How do they intertwine with the world-affirming expressions?**

Atheism

HEARING THE OTHER SIDE

Atheism as a set of beliefs is on the rise, and I suspect its ideas nibble each of us from time to time. The other morning I had coffee with my former college roommate. His dream in college was to become a minister, and he made that dream a reality. Then, after thirty years of ministry, he took early retirement in Florida as a professed atheist.

Two sips into his coffee, he became a prosecutor. "I no longer believe in talking snakes, Paul, or respect any God so dumb as to put the best fruit tree in the middle of a garden and expect a *Do Not Eat* sign would do anything but entice. Then your God turns hateful, condemning the human race because the first couple ate an apple. Vengefully, God restructures the earth so that women suffer in childbirth, men have to work and toil, and death is the fate of everything. Finally your God's anger cools, and God decides to send Jesus, a supposedly beloved son, to solve all our problems through his own violent death. The only hope we are given is to carry, like Jesus, our own tailor-made cross. If we sacrifice enough, God might forgive us for the inescapable sin caused by the Fall. And if we fail to gain forgiveness, God has a sadistic solution prepared called hell. Folks like me will be tortured forever there, while folks like you are predestined to cheer this grisly show from the balcony of heaven. Paul, this is nasty stuff, and I refuse to believe it."

Such an encounter is sobering, especially in knowing that his version squares with what some missionaries preached as conquistadors ravished the Aztecs and as troops herded Native Americans along the Trail of Tears. In fact, if this literalism is obligatory for being a Christian, I will join him gladly in sunny Florida.

"However you handle the talking snake bit," I replied, "the Eden story is right on. There is a threshold in God's evolutionary process when humans become self-conscious, and we are gifted with the freedom that I call the three C's. *Creativity* is the ability to imagine more than is. *Choice* is the freedom to picture possible actions before deciding. *Conscience* arises in feeling what the recipient of our possible actions would feel. With these abilities, we are enabled to accept God's call to move the earth into completeness.

"Yet in being created like God, there comes the temptation to be God. The three C's can become the three P's: the craving for *possessions,* *power,* and *prestige.* Adam thinks he hears a whisper: 'Who is God to order you around? Why isn't God out here helping with the plowing? If you were God, you could own this whole place for yourself.' Temptations begin as thoughts that build momentum and become actions. *Wouldn't that be something,* Adam ponders. *Power, prestige, possessions—all mine.*

"While *Adam* can mean 'first person,' I prefer the meaning of 'every person,' because through this story I understand both myself and history. The Fall reoccurs whenever God's dream of we, ours, and us, gets trampled by an obsession with I, me, and mine. In history, only the characters change—Cain and Abel, Abraham and Lot, Joseph and his brothers. Theologians call these contorted motives pride and concupiscence; I prefer ambition and appetite. These motives are the roots of sin.

"Our hope is in a crucified God who in Christ declares himself guilty for the sins we have done, even making excuses for his executioners and us, who 'know not what they do' (Luke 23:34, RSV). My friend, it is all about love. Three cheers for talking snakes."

My friend was quiet. Then he smiled, and ordered what he called "Eucharist donuts."

→ **What parts of my friend's criticism of Christianity are worth your wrestling? How would you respond to him from your own faith perspective?**

Baptism

MAKING THE PLUNGE

Many of us cannot recall our baptisms, even though they were our entry into Christian life. The early church appropriately chose the season of Lent for preparation. Early accounts speak emotionally of this baptismal rebirth at Easter as being helplessly plunged three times into the watery tomb of Christ's three-day death, then raised "breathlessly and triumphantly" into an Easter life extending into eternity. So thorough was this intended transformation that each person was renamed for a martyr and clothed in a white gown. Protestant revivals retain some of this drama by imagining that baptism is being washed in the blood of the Lamb.

Yet plunging rarely takes place in today's mainline churches. A domesticated infant baptism is the preferred method, where adoring parents introduce their infant to a smiling congregation. The baptism of our youth is likely less important than acquiring a driver's license. For adults, it is on a par with joining some civic organization. How tame this is in contrast to the original meaning of baptism as a primal event that renders a person subversive, declaring as secondary every other allegiance, alliance, goal, and dream. The tombstone is rolled away, disclosing an alternative world of definitive faithfulness to Christ alone.

In contrast to society's obsession with power, we are to die to ourselves in baptism. In resistance to society's obsession with possessions, we are not to store up for ourselves "treasures on earth" (Matt. 6:19). In disparaging society's worship of prestige, we are to become living proof that those who seek their lives will lose them, while those who relinquish their lives for Christ will truly find them. In conflict with a society that resorts to violence, Jesus models peace and a plea to love our enemies. Christian baptism pulls away disguises of our condition, unclothing our motives, defying appearances, and disclosing death as a lurking foe. With three backward baptismal plunges into Christ's death, our death dies, our future tomb empties, our debt is written off, and we rise up as persons released to new life.

Caught in the midst of warfare in Algeria, a community of seven Trappist monks discovered that baptism disqualified them from fleeing the country. As a sign of peace and reconciliation, they bonded their fate with the peasants they served and were in turn taken as hostages. When an earthly ransom was not forthcoming, their captors killed them. In a note found on his desk, the abbot asked forgiveness for any way in which he and his brothers might have unintentionally been accomplices to evil. Addressing his anticipated assassin, he prayed that at the moment of his death he would recognize in him the face of Christ. He wrote, "May you and I find each other as good thieves in Paradise." Immersion in martyrs' blood makes clear the meaning of our water immersion in Christ's crucifixion and resurrection, freeing us for participation in the world's Good Fridays as witness to their promised Easter.

⇥ **How might these stories from church tradition bring depth in better understanding your own baptism?**

Being Different

ON PURPOSE

Have you ever noticed that the harder we try to be spiritual, the more Jesus can be annoying? For example, he insists that our piety be invisible. It's difficult enough changing our habits without being told not to let a few friends know so that they can commiserate! But Jesus is unsympathetic to those of us whose motives for doing worthy things may be tainted by a desire to call attention to ourselves. When fasting we are not to let anyone know what we are doing, and when praying we should enter the closet and shut the door. So keen is Jesus on cleaning up our piety that he insists on our right hand never even suspecting what the left one is doing.

Not long ago I had lunch with a friend, and as was our custom, we gave quiet thanks for our food. With the "Amen," I opened my eyes and met the determined stare of a boy at the next table. With a public whisper only a child his age can master, he asked his mother, "What are they doing?" My piety had not passed the invisibility test.

Jesus lived in a society quite different from our own, where piety was appreciated and positively regarded. That is not our situation today. So can it be that in following Jesus' dictum about no public attention, we have actually forfeited practices that should differentiate us from our secular neighbors? The hymn "Ashamed of Jesus" is missing from mainline hymnals, but is there anything we Christians do today that could remotely bring us even the slightest shame?

Perhaps we might need to take a fresh look at Jesus' teaching. When piety was regarded as praiseworthy, persons were tempted to let it become visible for the wrong reasons. Only a hidden piety had much virtue. But in today's society, visible signs of piety would do the opposite, setting Christians apart with a difference risking embarrassment, if not disdain. Thus following Jesus' teaching about hiddenness in our changed environment might actually be a convenient way of internalizing our faith so that we can externally appear to be conformers. By becoming imperceptible Christians, we have an excuse to substitute a polite silence for sticking our necks out. We choose to fit in by forfeiting any public Christian identification, yet this might not be a faithful rendition of what Jesus had in mind but the opposite.

Whenever one finds it easy to obey the letter of one of Jesus' teachings, it is a strong clue that we may be violating its spirit—that is, doing the right thing for the wrong reason. At prescribed prayer times, many Muslims in this country stop whatever they are doing, no matter where they are, and roll out their prayer rugs. Instead of experiencing this behavior as ostentatious, I find it impressive that one's faith is strong enough to risk social disapproval. Since the intent of Jesus' teachings is to craft discipleship, obedience to the spirit of this teaching might entail doing the opposite of the letter. A virtuous piety would require today the courage to be seen as different. If nothing in our faith is cause for public embarrassment, is there much left in it worth bothering about?

This reversed application could involve only little things at first—such as wearing Ash Wednesday ashes long enough for a surprised colleague to offer a tissue. Or it might mean requesting a vacation day for a Christian observance like Good Friday. Or it could entail being resolute about keeping Sundays sacred. Or sending Christmas cards with a clear religious message. Or eating fish on Fridays. A good test for a possible action might be whether it would make us feel uncomfortable to be recognized as Christian. I admire the courage of a Jehovah's Witness in refusing to stand during the national anthem. We and the world need reminders that ours is a faith that makes a difference—by being a little different.

➤ **In what ways does being a Christian express itself recognizably in your living? What if you had more courage?**

Being Led

CROOKEDLY

Have you ever looked back on your life's wanderings and wished that God had kept the promise to "make straight the crooked paths" (Isa. 45:2, KJV)? Israel felt that way, wandering aimlessly in the desert for forty years, apparently going nowhere. But the following popular maxim illumines God's strange understanding of the word *straight*: "God writes straight with crooked lines." In my own life, it seems that if there were a path from where I began to where I am, it was hidden in a maze of zigzagged lines, unclear intersections, and apparent dead ends. But thankfully I am coming to recognize that my crooked lines have been God's straight ones. I have been led.

Strange as this sounds, and as contradictory as it is to what I have long thought, I have never really made an important decision in my life. My pilgrimage has been one of doors opening, insights coming, possibilities happening, coincidences occurring, and barricades dissolving. Things didn't just happen, and saying I was lucky is a cop-out. I can no longer connect my past with my present in terms of my own resolve. I am where I never planned to be, going in a direction I had never before walked, by ways I never expected, through means I never anticipated. "He leadeth me; O blessed thought!" says the hymn. God smiles at those who think they know where they are going.

Perhaps as Christians we should stop using the word *decision*; *discernment* seems more accurate. God lures us more than coerces us and invites more than demands. Rather than obeying some preset divine will, the Christian is called to discern God's yearnings. We are led by hunches, longings, guesses, thirsts, and allurements. T. S. Eliot calls them "hints followed by guesses." John Wesley refers to them as "whispers of the soul." God guided Israel with a cloud by day and a fire by night (see Exod. 13:21). Christians today may mention something before them persuading, beckoning, inviting, encouraging, leading, motivating, inspiring, stirring, arousing, provoking, inciting, awakening, or enticing. And when not before them, that something is behind snipping at heels and closing doors. Hound of heaven is its name.

How often we use the expressions "taken by surprise," "against my will," "when I least expected it," "just when I was about to give up," "out of a clear blue sky," "for unknown reasons," "little did I know," "the timing was right," or "it was what I needed to hear." Through spiritual direction, we learn to recognize and name the Spirit's nudgings.

Was is by chance that Francis of Assisi showed up at church as the scripture reading happened to be about proclaiming the kingdom of God without "gold, or silver, or copper" (Matt. 10:9)? Was it circumstantial that Wesley showed up at Aldersgate on the particular night that Luther's preface to Paul's letter to the Romans was being read? God's fingertips are at the forward edge of each moment. Providence is a far more thankful name than luck or coincidence.

⚜ **Draw a time line of your life indicating the key junctures that have made the most difference. Did you feel God's leading at the time? Do you see God's leading now?**

Belonging

WHY THE CHURCH?

Belonging isn't easy. Anyone moving into a rural community learns that quickly. The local postmaster introduced me recently to another customer. "He's a newcomer," the postmaster said.

"When did you move here?" I asked innocently.

"Five years ago," the "newcomer" replied.

In my community there are probably no more than three families who have lived in the town long enough to claim squatter's rights. Moving and displacement are even more prevalent in urban apartment housing and suburban condominiums, making feeling a sense of belonging increasingly unlikely. It is no surprise that the reason most given by persons for choosing a church is "I feel like I belong there."

Belonging, however, is far more than a church growth strategy; it is the defining nature of the church. Baptism is adoption into the family of God, and confirmation is an oath. While this oath is similar to what an immigrant takes in being granted citizenship, in this case, one consents to having already been incorporated through baptism into the body of Christ. Eucharist is the family meal that nurtures our oneness through a common loaf and shared cup. These acts make the church unique. Through baptism, confirmation, and Holy Communion, we are grafted onto a living vine. Or, using the analogy of a human organism, we become an indispensable and living part of the body of Christ, whether we function as heart, ear, lung, finger, or toenail.

Saint Paul tells us that this bonding is so complete that the sorrow of one person is the sadness of all, and the joy of any is the happiness of each. Scripture provides rich imagery for this sense of belonging;

we are called the "household of God," the "fellowship of believers," the "community of saints." Other strong words convey such a belonging: *incorporate, amalgamate, merge, unite, bond.* How deeply contrasting are these words to society's insistence on the individual as its defining unit, thereby isolating persons and the nuclear family to a lonely fending. Society, therefore, sees church as simply being one more voluntary group among many that may be joined, this one providing a supplemental religious dimension for those so inclined.

Christian life is thoroughly communal, for being in Christ means that we are in it together unto death and beyond. Thus at the heart of each church is a core of persons vowed to a countercultural lifestyle at odds with an individualistic society. As organically both divine and human, the church has used a beautiful image to express this—the Holy Mother church. Certainly the church is human, with a goodly collection of hypocrites and sinners. Yet just as essentially is she divine—consecrated by Christ as his body on earth so that "the gates of Hades will not prevail against it" (Matt. 16:18). Gregory of Nyssa deepens this analogy with the idea of the church as nurse, its teachings being our milk, its sacraments our food.

Worship is at the center of the church's communal life. While it may not always be clear what the shabby little church across town is all about, be assured that it is an invitation touching our deepest yearning—to be embraced in an organic belonging that God intends for the church to provide.

☙ In what ways does your local church provide the kind of belonging for which you yearn? How can the church offer this belonging to those outside its walls?

Black Sheep

WITHOUT AND WITHIN

Is there any family without at least one so-called black sheep? I stumbled upon my family's quite innocently over a year ago. My cousin Bill and I decided to work together to preserve much of our family's history lest it be lost. Teasing out stories from the fading memories of remaining relatives was more difficult than we imagined, especially as there began to emerge a mysterious gap that resisted filling. The gap had a name: Aunt Elizabeth. All that my father ever said was that one of his sisters "died early." By piecing together the sparse fragments, we began detecting dim contours of our family's black sheep.

As it turned out, when my grandmother died quite young, eldest daughter Elizabeth dropped out of school and for ten years was the surrogate mother for her six siblings. Still unmarried at age twenty-six, she found herself pregnant. Her father—my grandfather—heaped severe, perhaps alcohol-induced, abuse upon her. When Elizabeth contracted pneumonia, he refused to get a doctor and denied her assistance in delivering her stillborn child. When she promptly died, he had her buried in an unmarked grave, vowing with a curse that it would remain unmarked forever.

My grandfather is long dead, as are all of Aunt Elizabeth's brothers and sisters, including my father. But we had unearthed a spiritual cancer covered by years of denial. Was it too late to receive her into the family after such an exile? My cousin, an evangelical minister, sent me this prayer: "Elizabeth, I pray that someone during those sad hours and days said to you, 'God loves you.' May you have heard the God whisper, 'Come, my lovely one. The winter is past. Come, my beautiful one, come.' I cannot imagine otherwise." After months of searching, we finally found her grave and the grave of her nameless child. One bright spring morning, we placed and blessed a tombstone declaring her grave to be an adjunct family plot. Then I visited the graves of the relatives, explaining one by one the family reconciliation that had just happened. It is finished.

In sharing this story with friends, I was amazed by how many of them had their own black sheep. As we shared tears, it became clear that there is a black sheepness deep in each of us. The words of Jesus offer us redemption: "There is nothing covered that will not be revealed, and hidden that will not be known" (Matt. 10:26, NKJV).

⋙ **Do you know any black sheep? Have you been one?**

Bottoms

WHEN THEY FALL OUT

When persons come forward to receive Holy Communion, I look into their eyes to see if they understand Easter as resurrection. A slight smile, a knowing glance, or a moist eye hints that they get it. I feel that until the bottom gets knocked out of our lives, it is difficult for us to embrace the gift of Easter. Those who have experienced the sadness woven into life's fabric—sickness, loss, yearning, loneliness, fear, and death—understand the importance of Easter. The childhood memory of my aunt trying to pull my uncle out of his coffin, forcing his eyes open with a scream, "Speak to me!" remains vivid to this day. I heard a parishioner overcome with grief after her husband's death sob, "He promised not to leave without me."

Death seems final. No wonder the disciples couldn't believe the unbelievable. Resurrection rumors could only be idle talk. Even after seeing the empty tomb, Mary Magdalene drew the only reasonable conclusion: someone stole Jesus' body. Yet, the disciples did learn to believe, and they shared the story of a resurrected Christ with others. Peter and John were arrested for their beliefs. But why incarcerate a handful of broken peasants for saying they saw a dead man walk through their locked door? If a stranger told me he drank coffee with someone I saw being buried, I would offer directions to the psychiatric hospital, keeping walking, and advise friends to avoid him. But have him arrested? Hardly!

The arrests, threats, and whippings were not for telling tall tales. The civil and religious authorities responsible for keeping order were frightened. These simple men had been no threat while traipsing after a man who spoke of meekness, patience, and love. But once the few followers became crowds of people, the authorities made a crucified spectacle of Jesus. His disciples ran for cover, huddling fearfully behind locked doors.

No, the most powerful case for Easter is the resuscitation of hope from hopelessness. Such hope is what made the leaders edgy. "When they saw the boldness of Peter and John and realized that they were uneducated and ordinary men, they were amazed" (Acts 4:13). No, they were startled—at what seemed threateningly miraculous. They asked, "By what power or by what name did you do this?" (Acts 4:7). These poor, broken, hopeless outcasts were standing fearlessly before the leaders of their time—no longer harmless riffraff but commanding men with unbelievable poise, power, certainty, and conviction. In the disciples' strength, the authorities beheld the very one they had executed, who challenged the powers and principalities with a rival authority. The issue is not what the disciples believed but what happened when they did believe.

Preserving social order depends on instilling a fear of punishment, but these disciples were fearless of everything the authorities could do. Such insubordination has all the hallmarks of treason. "For freedom Christ has set us free" (Gal. 5:1). When imprisonment failed, persecution began. When that proved counterproductive, extermination was the order. And ever since, Christians have modeled for the world what it means to be resurrection—fearless before threat, joyous under intimidation, and glorious in martyrdom.

The evidence for Easter remains the same today. *Resurrection* means being "born again" after the bottom falls out. Truth of the Resurrection hangs daily in the balance, tested by the willingness of Christians to live and die as Christ for others.

⤙ **What parallels do you see between the resurrection of the disciples and your own response when the bottom has threatened to fall out of your life?**

Bragging

ABOUT OUR WEAKNESSES

All of us learn early in our lives how to brag. Even if I didn't have much to brag about, I could always say, "My dad can beat your dad!" In time our stories become more expansive—from the impressive size of the fish we didn't quite catch, to golf scores that are more or less correct. School reunions can exercise our penchants for bragging while family reunions provide less opportunity, for relatives have less than grandiose memories of us.

Society molds us to compete in almost everything. We are encouraged to win and to be the best. Aggressiveness and ambition are encouraged traits, giving acclaim to whoever places first and awarding with more those who have most. To be last in anything is failure.

Jesus reverses this idea by insisting that the first shall be last, apparently having already signed the deed for the meek to inherit the earth. In faithful response, Saint Paul developed an intriguing way of responding to local church bragging to be first. Here are the activities about which Paul could boast: hard labor, imprisonment, near-death experiences, lashings, beatings, shipwrecks, countless stonings, homelessness, floods, robbers, betrayal, sleepless nights, hunger, thirst, frostbite, nakedness, and daily anxiety. "If I must boast," Paul writes, "I will boast of the things that show my weakness" (2 Cor. 11:30).

What are we to make of this "reverse bragging," this contest of failures rather than of accomplishments? Wouldn't it mark the end of Christianity if the church were to develop an evangelistic campaign brochure using Paul's list as reasons for becoming a Christian? Yet these are the characteristics that scripture applauds as authentic marks of being Christian—and society considers the very marks of failure. When God does not function as our god, we squander our lives by trying for fifteen minutes of public applause. But God's ongoing love refuses to be tender towards whatever keeps us from being genuine. So the psalmists acknowledge that authentic life is born by undergoing times when only God can sustain us.

This is how Paul came to realize what makes it possible to brag about our weaknesses, vulnerabilities, and finitude: a gift from God. "Whenever I am weak, then I am strong" (2 Cor. 12:10). How can we find joy in God's gift? Hints of such joy can surface when the threat of cancer evokes a daily thankfulness for whatever time one has, or when in suffering abandonment one finds stability in the thought of the lost sheep and the ninety-nine, or when death's inevitability evokes the promise of resurrection and new life. When we are no longer anxiously fixated on making something of ourselves, we are opened for God's use—as success or as failure. That is when we "will be free indeed" (John 8:36).

⇥ **Identify specifically the kinds of recognition that feed you. Which of these needs might better be served by practicing Paul's approach to bragging?**

Called

AS CALLING

During confirmation, we face two fundamental questions: To whom do I give my life? To what do I give my life? Yet first we acknowledge that we are not really free to give ourselves away because we have already given our lives in baptism. We were bought by Christ and claimed for life. In confirmation, we commit ourselves to discerning through the guidance of the Holy Spirit our unique vocational calling. We become servants to the world in Christ's name. The church affirms this aspect of confirmation by marking the person with the same oil used in ordaining priests and ministers. John Henry Newman affirmed this personally: "God has created me to do Him some definite service. He has committed some work to me which He has not committed to another. I have my mission." Precisely to what calling we give our lives may not be known, but during confirmation, we commit ourselves to the search.

As a teenager, I attended church camp one summer. There, around a roaring campfire, wrapped in rhythmic singing, the leader called forward those who felt called to full-time Christian service. I came forward. With a huge hug he expressed happiness that I was going to be a minister. "No, sir," I replied. "I am going to be a Christian doctor." With a scowl, I was escorted back into the darkness, made to understand that I had misunderstood the question. Not until I read Martin Luther in graduate school did I discover that I had been right. Luther insisted that each Christian is called by God to a particular work, whether that be as a lawyer, teacher, mechanic, whatever. Confirmation is our commitment to the process of discerning our roles in the kingdom of God. "Whatever you do, do everything for the glory of God" (1 Cor. 10:31).

This entails differentiating between doing what I might want to do and doing what God is calling me to do. And openness to have God working through me goes beyond doing work for God.

The distinction between a job and a calling is radical. Most Christians would agree that we are called to be Christlike in our vocations, employing the Golden Rule to work honestly, conscientiously, and with care. But John Calvin pushes that calling a step further—to be Christled through our vocations. There is a considerable contrast between a Christian who is a doctor and a Christian doctor. The former would care about patients, while the latter would question medical practices that place profit above healing. A Christian banker not only would be fair in her dealings but also would oppose unfair business practices. A Christian teacher would care for the students but would also challenge the equivocation of learning and testing.

When one moves to a different living location, a major problem is finding persons who can be trusted to provide vital services. I was blessed to find a Christian garage mechanic whose shop was marked by a modest sign with a picture of Jesus and these few words: *This person supervises our work.* I felt the same satisfaction in discovering a Mennonite carpenter. Many churches have liturgies that remind us to "Remember your baptism and be thankful." In addition, we need a liturgy that reminds us to "Remember your confirmation by acknowledging your calling." This means that local churches would commission Christian plumbers, lawyers, parents, teachers, nurses, therapists, and so on. "In the midst of a crooked and perverse generation" of self-serving profiteering, persons living and sharing their Christian faith "shine like stars in the world" (Phil. 2:15).

→ **What changes would occur in your life if you began to understand your life in terms of calling? Are you willing to make these changes?**

Chosen

NOT TO CHOOSE

*J*esus said, "You did not choose me but I chose you" (John 15:16). This statement could ruffle some feathers because we always want to be the ones doing the choosing. Providing choices has become a marketable asset, from the supermarket's staggering array of options to the infinite amount of choices we make each day concerning what we will eat, wear, and visit. Inversely, not being chosen can have its negative sides. A humiliating childhood memory concerns recess when I was the last kid chosen for a team activity. Worse than being chosen last, I felt merely tolerated by my teammates.

Our desire to be chosen is why Gospel stories such as the parable of the ninety-nine sheep are so powerful for many of us. Jesus left all the rest and came looking for me! Amazing things happen when Jesus calls a person by name. To be named is to be called; to be called is to be chosen; to be chosen is to be claimed. When Peter, James, and John heard their names, each of them immediately abandoned what they were about, all that they had, and whom they had become. Jesus has this uncanny ability to make a person feel chosen.

I still cherish the day when one of my five daughters said, "Pops, I know you love us all, but somehow you make each of us feel special." As God's children, we are inimitably created, uniquely loved, and wonderfully esteemed. Grace is the name for God's matchless capacity to choose in a manner that is exclusively inclusive.

To drive home the incredibleness of this special companionship that God has for each of us, Paul is not content simply to claim that God does the choosing. God's love is so great that "he chose us in Christ before the foundation of the world" (Eph. 1:4). Predestination is the theological name—and many Christians find this term offensive. This is understandable if the God who is doing the predestining is the one Jonathan Edwards portrayed in his frightening sermon titled, "Sinners in the Hands of an Angry God." But what if predestining is the insistence that being uniquely loved by God is not something that the few might attain as a competitive award for scoring *summa cum laude* on life's final exam? Rather, our eternal destiny rests in the hands of the God who even before we were born so loved us that he died our death. With such a God as this, being chosen suddenly becomes good news. Thus even Calvin, known for his insistence on predestination, prayed hopefully that such a God chooses us all. "We have our hope set on the living God, who is the Savior of all people, especially of those who believe" (1 Tim. 4:10).

➤ **Name a particularly painful time in your life when you were not chosen. What changes when you remember that experience as if you are not alone but with Jesus, who has chosen you as his special friend?**

Christianity

NOT AN ETHIC

Required by my parents to attend church for eighteen years, I became quite a connoisseur of sermons. In content, most preachers agreed with Isaiah: "Maintain justice, and do what is right" (Isa. 56:1). So while the message stressed the doing, it missed the reason for the doing, the why. For the Christian, the answer to this question focuses not on our doing but on God's. The early church did not reject law but instead reversed its function. Rather than disclosing what we are to do, the law reveals what we are incapable of doing. Therefore, Christianity is a religion not of ethics but of salvation and healing. I believe in the mantra, "I can't, but God can." This is not to say that we shouldn't do good things but that the good we do tends to be for the wrong reasons. The dilemma has to do with motivation. There is a why for everything we do, and what that why is makes the difference.

The Christian diagnosis begins in recognizing that we are created with a deep need to be loved. There are two radically different kinds of love: conditional and unconditional. Conditional love involves bargaining, and there are conditions that we must meet in order to receive love from others. By definition, then, our motivation is self-interest—doing in order to receive. Such conditional living is exhausting, involving a treadmill of constant doing in order to earn and maintain love. But beneath such doing lurks the anxiety that we can never do enough, or do it well enough, or be lovable enough in the eyes of others. And yet we dare not stop. Even our worship is tainted—rather than being for God, we participate in worship in order to get something out of it.

Unconditional love is radically different, involving a conversion of our motives. The Christian dynamic is "not that we loved God but that he loved us" (1 John 4:10). Unconditional love is a gift in which the initiative is God's and not ours, beginning "while we still were sinners" (Rom. 5:8). Our prior motivation of receiving is replaced by gratitude in response to having received the love that we have always craved. Human love always expects something in return, yet God's love does not. Grace is the name for God's incredible love, making our games of calculated conditionality appear childish. God loves us because of who God is, not because of who we are or have done. Instead, we are freed to love as we are loved.

To illustrate, conditional love expressed toward a wayward daughter would say, "Jane, unless you start behaving properly, I've had it with you!" Only if she meets my conditions will I show her love. Unconditional love says, "Jane, I love you so deeply that nothing can ever break that love. That is why we need to talk!" The syntax is not *if* or *then* but *because* and *therefore*. Rather than doing in order to receive, our doing is the thankful response for having received. Thus even the Golden Rule is radicalized: Love your neighbor as you have been loved by Christ.

➤ **Reflect on a time when you felt genuinely loved. By whom? How was it akin to God's love? How did it differ?**

Covenant

GIVING UP ON US?

*I*n exploring our relationship with God, the biblical concept of *covenant* becomes essential. The word differs greatly from *contract*, which is a mutual agreement that remains valid only as long as both parties uphold their parts. Covenant involves the idea of bonding, as in the case with Israel, to whom God said, "I will take you as my people, and I will be your God" (Exod. 6:7). Through its long history, Israel came to realize the implications of covenant; a covenant with God is permanent and unbreakable. This is why scripture uses the analogy of marriage to describe this Divine-human relationship. But as divorce rates have risen in our society, marriage has been reduced from covenant to contract. This makes marriage a problematic analogy for understanding our covenantal relationship with God.

To regain its fuller meaning, it is helpful to observe the evolution that occurs in the Hebrew scriptures as God makes and remakes a series of covenants with Abraham, Noah, Moses, and Jeremiah. At times, God considers breaking the covenants, and the prophets portray a God growing increasingly weary of being the only faithful partner in the covenant. But with Hosea, Israel passes over a threshold in covenantal understanding. Hosea is led to discern how deeply God's covenant is rooted in love, so much so that when Israel is unfaithful, God is heartbroken. God's initial impulse is divorce, acting as if the relationship were a violated contract rather than a covenant. For a moment God tries to break it—but can't. God simply cannot give up beloved Israel. This totally transcends any idea of a contract. We have a covenant with God—all the way, at soul depth.

From this point on, covenant means being claimed by God's definitive promise rooted forever in the ultimate love affair. No matter how much God is angered by Israel's faithlessness, God will not, cannot, walk away. So grounded and rooted in love, the psalmists can express without hopelessness God's horrorstruck agony over how a chosen people "defiled themselves by their deeds and broke their marriage bond with the Lord" (Ps. 106:39, *The Psalms*). Hope remains, always, and it is this: "God remembered for their sake his covenant, and relented according to the abundance of his steadfast love" (Ps. 106:45, RSV).

Impressive as this relationship is, it turns out to be only a foretaste. In Jesus Christ this covenant is broadened. The covenant with Israel now includes the entire human race: "[Jesus] is the atoning sacrifice for our sins, and not for ours only but also for the sins of the whole world" (1 John 2:2). Even more, God not only expands the covenant but also becomes it. Jesus Christ—fully God and fully human—offers the promise of resurrection for everyone. Through Jesus Christ, this covenant was signed—with water and in blood.

➤ In what ways is your relationship with God contractual? In what ways is it covenantal? When have you wanted to get out of the relationship? When have you wanted to stay in?

Days After

WITH INVISIBILITY

The days after both Christmas and Easter are personal letdowns. On these days, life returns to normal, and we may feel as if we are no longer seen or cared for. This feeling of loneliness and anonymity is the test of faith. Let me explain. One day at the monastery I was assigned to clean a room that is rarely used or even entered. Vacuuming made little sense, much less pulling out boxes to vacuum behind them. No one would ever see, know, or care about the work I had done. All alone in that forgotten room, I began to realize how much my daily doing is done in order to be seen, recognized, acknowledged, or praised. If floors are to be shined, sinks scrubbed, walls painted, let it be known who did it—me!

I sat down, right there in the middle of the dusty floor, slowly feeling condemned by how work and chores in the monastery are performed anonymously. Laundry gets done, dishes are put away, groceries appear, tubs are cleaned, and sugar bowls are miraculously filled. All of this happens as if by magic. I began to realize that a keen indicator of how far one has come in the process of becoming Christian is the willingness to be anonymous, delighted to do secretly the humblest of tasks as if only to please God. Saint Paul finally came to this understanding: "Whatever you do, do your work heartily, as for the Lord rather than for men" (Col. 3:23, NASB). Blessed are those who, when no one is around to care, continue to do good to the glory of God.

Thérèse of Lisieux strove for this purity of anonymity by hoping that her acts of love would be surprises even for God. We can never be saints if we are conscious of acting saintlike. Therefore let us nominate for sainthood those nameless workers who are content to be "hidden with Christ in God" (Col. 3:3), doing well whatever needs doing just because. By the way, I did vacuum behind the boxes. *LoL*

➤ **In considering whether to do some difficult action, what difference would it make if you knew for certain that no one would see or ever know you did it?**

Diversity of Perspectives

THEOLOGICAL WORLDS

None of us would likely be serious Christians if we had not endured a deep need that Christ was able to touch. To be a Christian is to affirm, as the hymn "I Love to Tell the Story" claims, that he "satisfies my longing as nothing else can do." While there is a common human condition that we all face, each of us experiences our humanity a bit differently. The differences in the four Gospels are rooted in the differences of the authors' personal needs, which accounts as well for the variety of denominations, the disagreements between theologians, and the range of believers from liberal to conservative. Therefore the church dare not insist on there being one mandatory perspective for all believers. The need, instead, is to encourage faithful creativity by establishing broad channel markers sufficient to inhibit invalidation on the one hand and dilution on the other. Jesus speaks of "the narrow gate" (Matt. 7:13), yet treats each person as one of a kind.

In providing spiritual direction, I have developed a typology of five alternative ways in which Christians tend to experience the human condition and deal with it. First, there are persons whose deep longing is shaped by the feeling of separation or abandonment, experienced as not belonging. This may be evoked by a range of circumstances, from feeling interpersonal distance to a sense of lostness in the enormity of the cosmos. As aliens, they desire reunion, homecoming, and belonging. These persons tend to find their answer in Christ as *Revealer*, enabling a mysticlike foretaste of union: "That they may be one even as we are one, I in them and thou in me, that they may become perfectly one" (John 17:22-23, RSV).

Second are persons who are distressed by the oppressive condition of the world and conflicted by injustice, suffering, and death. Feeling like warriors, their yearning is for Christ as *Liberator*, as the one who takes sides in vindicating the poor, the rejected, and the dead. They eagerly await the promise of a new heaven and new earth. Third are those who ache from a sense of emptiness deep inside, giving to them the feeling of being an outcast, of not measuring up. The Christ to whom they are drawn personifies a wholeness birthed by the gift of unconditional love. Christ is *Lover*.

Fourth are those claimed by a sense of guilt, stained not only by what they have done but by who they are. Feeling like fugitives, these persons yearn for Christ as *Savior*, one who pays the price to gain our undeserved forgiveness, wiping clean the slate. Fifth are those feeling overwhelmed by life, who feel like helpless victims. They need Christ as *Suffering Servant*, a companion closer than life itself with whom to endure long-suffering. "Even though I walk through the darkest valley, I fear no evil; for you are with me" (Ps. 23:4).

One of these plots likely identifies the theological spectrum in which a person lives and moves and understands the world. The church needs to respect this diversity, presenting a multifaceted Christ capable of satisfying the particularized longings of each person. This can be helped by providing alternative worship services structured, in turn, by the theology of each world; and offering alternative supportive accountability groups in which persons can find others with whom to share their lives. When persons are fed and bonded in such diverse ways within an overarching congregation, cross-fertilization occurs, inviting persons to be amenable to other Christian versions, curing us of the tendency to impose our own worldviews on everyone.

➵ **In which theological world do you live? How do these theology types help you relate to others?**

Doing More

THAN GETTING IT DONE

*J*esus doesn't seem overly impressed by the good acts we perform. In fact, among his final teachings comes this declaration: "When you have done all that is commanded you, say, 'We are unworthy servants; we have only done what was our duty'" (Luke 17:10, RSV). Why, he asks, should folks be praised simply for doing what they are supposed to do?

We might say, "I go to church almost every Sunday," or "I am a member of the Parish Council," or "I teach Sunday school." So what? says Jesus. By not being impressed, Jesus exposes much of our piety as motivated by a desire for recognition. Jesus believes that these are things Christians ought to do out of duty, never expecting to be asked, thanked, or praised.

Parents living with a teenager can certainly understand this perspective. If something is left in the hallway over which anyone could easily trip, our son or daughter simply walks around it. "Why didn't you pick it up?" we ask the child. "You didn't tell me to!" "You shouldn't have to be told!" Doing our duty is not even enough. Why not?

I had an older fourth-grade teacher named Mrs. Howe. One of the duties befalling us boys was to take the chalkboard erasers down to the boiler room, open the flue, and pound the chalk dust out of them. Under pressure, we dutifully took our turns, but none of us ever volunteered for the task. Mrs. Howe became quite ill, and a young Miss Penrod took her place. We boys immediately fell in love with her. "Who would like to clean the erasers for me?" she asked. Shouts came from all around the room. We all wanted to complete the task. Whomever she chose, the rest of us would shout, "It's not fair; Charlie got to do it last week!" What was the incredible difference? With Mrs. Howe, our obedience was motivated by duty. But with Miss Penrod, being in love made everything different. With duty, one does only what one has to do. With love, one can never do enough. So it is in church. Many of us act out of duty, because someone has to do the work. But there are others, the hidden saints, about whom Jesus has a good word. Acting out of love, they have no need to be told to perform the duty or praised for doing it.

→ **Where have you experienced parallels in your life to the dynamics of my fourth-grade classroom? What insight does this provide for improving your motivation?**

Envy

AND SELF-IMAGE

Are there any of us who never experience envy? The Adam and Eve story provides an uncomfortable mirror to our own desires. Being like God easily slid into wanting to be God. We all look to others as models for our own lives, but envy is different. Rather than a desire to emulate persons, envy begins as covetousness—the desire to possess what they have, take it away, leave them without. The slope of feeling envy and acting on this envy is so slippery that Jesus treats the two as nearly identical. The one who lusts "has already committed adultery with her in his heart" (Matt. 5:28), for the desire lacks only the opportunity. One who envies is on the edge of jealousy and subsequently hatred.

Envy's dynamic originates in the struggle we all have with low self-image. We tend not to like who we are, resenting the hand we have been dealt. Envy is birthed in not wanting to be who we are. "Why can't I be . . . ?" or "If only I were . . ." Instead of becoming better versions of ourselves, we foster resentment over who we are not. Our competitive society renders this consequence almost inevitable. Classrooms, halls, gymnasiums, auditoriums—these are our early crucibles forging competition. The smartest, the most athletic, the most popular; the player of the game, the employee of the week, the student of the month. If we cannot be first, we envy the one who is. Envy can easily become finding satisfaction in the failures and pains of others. Kierkegaard was right— love and comparison are mutually exclusive.

The gospel needs to be radical stuff to empower us into living outside the powerful forces of envy and jealousy. Our cure begins by realizing that God intends us to be precisely who we are. No matter how much I try to become someone else, there remains a sacredly indelible me beneath it all, someone who is cherished by God and unlike any other person ever created.

This realization is the converting moment. Jesus insists that only in discarding the false selves that we wanted to be can we uncover the real selves that God created us to become. When the pretense of being who we are not is punctured, we experience the gift of being one-of-a-kind, wanting nothing other than to be our own version of God's own image. We are contented with our unique selves, excited to become the person God always had in mind.

>* **Honestly, do you like who you are? Do you fantasize about being someone else? How does it feel to know that God chose you to be who you are?**

Evangelism

WITH OUR WITHOUT WORDS

God is able to achieve God's own will regardless of what obstacles we manage to build. Take the book of Acts, for example. When persecution attempted to obliterate the fledgling group of Christians, they resisted intimidation and instead showed a heroic amount of courage. As intensified persecution caused the Christians to leave Jerusalem, they took the good news enthusiastically with them. The resulting evangelism became so widespread and effective that it took on the semblance of a divine master plan.

An analogy would be if a large congregation disperses its members into every town in the area, each person committed to living the gospel intensely—in character, speech, appearance, work, play, and relationships. As neighbors become intrigued by this different way of living, they are invited into one's home for a fellowship of bread and wine, sharing in depth the problems and hopes of their lives. This illustrates the heart of evangelism then and now. It is a matter of contagion through enthusiasm. Evangelism today takes a bad rap because it is shifting from the Gospel analogies of fishing, feeding, and shepherding to the calculated scheming that characterizes the advertising industry.

The college dorm in which I lived was a large house. The third floor, once a ballroom, was our dormitory. Nighttime was like a zoo, as each of the twenty of us stumbled up the dark stairs to bed at vastly different times. One late night when all but one of us were finally asleep, the door suddenly burst open. Up the stairs a roommate raced, fresh from a late movie. Flipping on all the lights, he bellowed with a thunderous voice, "You've got to see it! It's awesome!" Pillows flew at him from all directions, yet he persevered, bouncing on his bed in a determination to give us a blow-by-blow.

"Tell us in the morning!" we cried.

But impervious to all our pleading, he persisted, "It's too good to keep!" Upset as we were with him, the truth is that within a week we had all gone to see the movie.

That is what evangelism is about—an inner insistence on sharing what is "too good to keep." It has nothing to do with arguing, threatening, or intimidating. Only resentment would have resulted if our roommate had said, "Unless you go to see that movie, I won't have anything more to do with you!" Evangelism at its heart is always positive—a wishing for others the joy of that with which one has been gifted. Evangelism adopts St. Francis's method of preaching the love of Jesus, sometimes even using words.

☞ **What is something—an activity, song, or book—that makes you enthusiastic? How do you express your enthusiasm to others?**

Evil

WHOSE IDEA WAS IT?

Most of us have been haunted by the existence of evil. Because of it, much of my life has been a wavering on the knife-edge between Christianity and atheism. How can there be a God when illness ends lives too soon, natural disasters devastate families, violence takes innocent lives, and suicides blot out those who can find no other way? The cartoon character Ziggy speaks for me as he pleads toward heaven: "Sir, have you noticed that the meek are still getting creamed?" How can one love a God who designed a world where death, sickness, war, and destruction seem to have the last word?

Job is the central scriptural portrait of this problem. Through no fault of his own, Job, a good and honest man, is stripped of everything—his family, his wealth, even his health. Job demands a trial to present his case. The evidence is heavy that God has a gambling problem, addicted to rolling the dice each morning to determine the day's allotment of tragedies.

Yet under God's painful cross-examination, Job is humbled by the mystery of creation. "Where were you when I laid the foundation of the earth?" God inquires (Job 38:4). After such an indictment, Job is left to trust that a Creator so amazing must have a plan even if he doesn't understand what it is. That might have been enough for Job but not me. Pain, suffering, and death are woven into the very fabric of creation.

Let me be painfully personal. My father died from cancer several months after my mother succumbed to her own death from the fear of having to live without him. At the visitation, friends offered solace with variations on the theme of how comforting it must be that God called my father home. I barely endured that painful evening, finally making a hasty exit into the cold night to vomit into a dumpster. "God, what a horrible way to call someone home—by torturing him to death!" I cringed as a mortuary recording played Bach's "Come Sweet Death."

Sleepless that night in bed, I drew my own conclusion. If death is God's idea, I want no part of him! That lonely night I became gripped by Jesus' final night in Gethsemane—sweating drops of blood, falling on his face in fear, pleading three times to have death's cup taken from him. Death was no friend to Jesus, no kind welcome home. Jesus said to Peter, James, and John, "I am deeply grieved, even to death" (Mark 14:34). Come sweet death? No way. Jesus' death was terrifying, painful, cruel, wrenching from his lips a godforsaken scream of despair on behalf of all humanity. I realized then that Jesus, one way or the other, would be the answer to my primal question: Is death God's design, or is it God's foe?

If Jesus is only human, he is the tragic disclosure that God is my foe—and I will defy that God to my dying breath. But if I can point to the crucified Jesus and declare, "Behold your God," then that reverses everything. The cross is God struggling against death, taking sides against it, declaring it to be the enemy in all its sordid manifestations. "The last enemy to be destroyed is death" (1 Cor. 15:26), and Jesus Christ is God's commitment to have the last word. When the resurrected Christ appears to his disciples, the holes from the nails that pierced his body remain. Resurrection is God's ongoing promise to struggle with our Good Fridays. Our struggles are God's struggles too. The God who shall "wipe every tear from their eyes" (Rev. 21:4) is on our side. I wrapped my father in that promise.

➤ **What personal tragedy in your life has given you most cause to doubt? How has it affected the way you understand God? Is death a foe for you or a friend?**

Eucharist

I'LL DRINK TO THAT

Though Holy Communion is central to the Christian faith, it is not easy to explain. My family members do not share my faith and belief in God, yet at our Christmas gatherings, they insist on continuing a tradition we have neither missed nor explained. We pass a loaf of freshly baked bread, and as each person tears off a piece, he or she answers this question: "What would I like to have broken from my life this coming year?" Answers vary—impatience, anger, jealousy, self-doubt, gossiping, insecurity, control, self-aggrandizement, workaholism. To each comes the family response, "We're in it together." Then we pass a goblet of wine, which carries its own question: "What is your hope for this coming year?" Again, answers vary—from peace for the world, compassion toward others, to feeling more centered. We respond, "We will hope with you." Also, as each person holds the goblet, all of us in turn complete this sentence of blessing: "What you mean to me is . . ." Often with thankful tears, the person responds, "I'll drink to that!"

This is not the Eucharist, but it is powerfully eucharistic. In a formal Eucharist, the breaking of bread is understood as nailing a piece of one's brokenness onto Christ's cross, merged with the suffering and crucifixions of the whole world. As Jesus said, "And I, when I am lifted up from the earth, will draw all people to myself" (John 12:32). The wine of joy is a toast of resurrection in rebonding God's beloved community to his body. Truly we're in it together, seeing Christ in the face of one another.

The altar for our family event is the dining room table. Proverbs provides an apt image: "[Wisdom] has prepared her meat and mixed her wine; she has also set her table . . . She says, 'Come, eat my food and drink the wine I have mixed'" (9:2, 5, NIV). The psalmist provides the reason for such a feast: "Taste and see that the LORD is good" (Ps. 34:8). Saint Paul provides the refrain: "[Give] thanks to God the Father at all times and for everything in the name of our Lord Jesus Christ" (Eph. 5:20). Why? For starters, Jesus offers this promise: "Whoever eats of this bread will live forever" (John 6:51). I'll drink to that.

The word *feast* helps me understand the promise made by the Eucharist, but you may understand it through different analogies. *Banquet* is a good word, but I've endured too many after-dinner speeches. Maybe *reunion*? No, I remember Aunt Lizzie at the last one! Perhaps a *picnic* but without the flies. All these scenarios could work, but I think I'll stick with *feast* since it describes what I experience with my family. After expressing our hopes for the coming year, we enjoy a turkey dinner, during which each person shares the highs and lows of his or her year. It evokes for me the parable of the great dinner in which the host says to his servant, "Go out at once into the streets and lanes of the town and bring in the poor, the crippled, the blind, and the lame"—so that all may experience love and community (Luke 14:21).

Our Christmas ends with an embrace, with each saying to the others, "You are mine, and I am yours." What better way to echo Christ's command, "Abide in me as I abide in you" (John 15:4). I'll drink to that!

⤳ **What parallels in your life can deepen the meaning of Holy Communion?**

Failing

BIG TIME

Most of us have experienced undesired but necessary yearly reviews. At the monastery we schedule them every two years, and they are called a Visitation. During a Visitation, the abbot of our Mother House comes for a week to work and pray alongside the monks, interviewing each privately. Finally, with fear and trepidation, the community is assembled for the reading of the visitation card. This encounter recalls my younger days of reckoning when the teacher would hand out report cards to take home to our parents. Visitation cards are report cards for monks!

Scripture is God's visitation card to us. The prophets were especially hard graders. Take Isaiah's note to Israel: "Let the wicked forsake their way" (Isa. 55:7). Ezekiel did him one better: "When the righteous turn away from their righteousness and commit iniquity, they shall die for it" (Ezek. 18:26). That's the kind of grading likely to get one's attention. Yet in my teaching career it seemed that students were more receptive to correction if I began with a positive comment. In contrast, the scriptural approach appears to favor the opposite—telling the bad right up front.

Which way works best? I sympathize with Ezekiel's reaction to a negative grading card: "The LORD's way is not fair!" (Ezek. 18:29, NAB). Yet I recall flunking high school calculus mid-semester. I just didn't get it. Crushed, I walked home clutching the report card that declared to the whole world that I would never get it. Expecting the worse, I handed it to my mother. She looked sternly at the card and then at me. Then she reached out to me with a memory from her own past: "Honey, calculus is hard. I know." That was what I needed to hear. I passed the course.

The gospel is for those of us with spotty report cards, those of us who seem to be on our way to flunking spiritual calculus. As strange as it may sound, God's way of blessing us is to force open the book of our lives until, sufficiently chastened, we are able to write our own visitation card. Hope for God's honor roll begins with an awareness of failure. We are all damaged merchandise, and yet we begin our spiritual journeys with Jesus' command: "Be perfect, therefore, as your heavenly Father is perfect" (Matt. 5:48). Ever try being perfect? I can pull it off for about five minutes on a sunny day.

Therefore, in response to our imperfection, Jesus might write at the bottom of our report card, "You are unworthy, for you have only done what was your duty" (see Luke 17:10). There is writing on the back of the card, but before reading it, the psalmist helps us say the appropriate prayer: "Be mindful of your mercy, O LORD . . . . Do not remember the sins of my youth or my transgressions" (Ps. 25:6-7). Then we can turn over the card. After delivering God's harsh judgment, Isaiah writes on the back: "Our God, who is generous in forgiving" (Isa. 55:7, NAB). We would get it all wrong if we read the reverse side first. Scripture tells us that only when we acknowledge our need for forgiveness are we able to experience the heart of God. The turning points in our lives are not in getting it right but in suffering the consequences of having gotten it wrong. God is not tender toward that which is ruining us.

This may account for why "Amazing Grace" is the favorite all-time hymn. The song is the astonished witness of a repentant slave trader in discovering God's eagerness to forgive such "a wretch as I." Christianity is about being lost but found, fallen but raised, tainted but cleansed, sick but healed, arrogant but humbled, wrong but righted, guilty but forgiven, unlovable but loved. This is why Jesus said, "I have come to call not the righteous but sinners" (Matt. 9:13).

⇥ **Write your own visitation card—both sides.**

Faith

FROM WHY TO INTO

Seconds can change everything. The big bang, we are told, occurred in a split second, and, for Christians, the world's meaning was determined in the last moments of Jesus' life—that is, the amount of time it took for that infamous Friday to become Good. The scene is the Crucifixion. Jesus cried out, "My God, why have you forsaken me?" (Matt. 27:46). Forsaken us! The earth held its breath as "darkness came over the whole land" (Mark 15:33). And then, "the earth shook, and the rocks were split" (Matt. 27:51). But there is more. Jesus spoke with a loud voice, "Father, into your hands I commend my spirit" (Luke 23:46).

Truly it is finished, but in a very different sense. Having endured every rejection that the human condition can offer, the final words of Jesus defy logic. In spite of all evidence to the contrary, at the edge of death, Jesus is able to trust that God waits for him behind the fragile curtain that separates earth from heaven. Rejected, betrayed, and deserted, Jesus expresses final words of trust: "Into your hands . . ."

If it were not for Jesus, I would be an atheist. I cannot do what he did. Immersed in a world filled with suffering and death, I cannot trust what he trusted. Jesus' final words represent the chasm I cannot bridge. On my own, I cannot leap from *why* to *into*. I cannot. This is why I am a Christian.

Faith means trusting the Jesus who was able to trust God as Father. For better or worse, Jesus and I are in it together. A prayer from the breviary says it best: "Lord Jesus, you were rejected by your people, betrayed by the kiss of a friend, and deserted by your disciples. Give us the

confidence that you had in the Father, and our salvation will be assured"
(v. IV). Though I may have trouble directly trusting God, I trust Jesus.

➤ **Is the faith of Jesus central to your own ability to trust God? In
what way is Jesus essential to your own faith?**

Faith

NOT BELIEF

Martin Luther was greatly irritated by the writer of the book of James, which he labeled "an epistle of straw" hardly worth burning! Luther's anger was in defense of Paul's insistence that God initiates our redemption; we cannot initiate redemption on our own. While we are still sinners God offers us unmerited forgiveness. Forgiveness is a gift and not dependent on anything we do or deserve. So does the writer of James disagree? No. But he wants to test the authenticity of our faith by seeing if it results in caring for the poor, needy, and powerless. Surely Luther would agree. So what's the conflict? I think it resides in confusion over the differences between faith and belief.

Belief is no big deal, the writer of James insists. Even the demons believe in God. Belief means assenting that something is true. We believe all kinds of things. Faith, in contrast, means trusting a particular truth so that it significantly affects what we do. Thus, for the Christian, faith in Christ means exactly what Jesus describes in the book of Matthew. Jesus says, "If any want to become my followers, let them deny themselves and take up their cross and follow me" (Matt. 16:24). Faith involves more than believing about; it involves trusting in. Trusting in Christ means a total surrender of your life by living as a disciple.

This faith-versus-belief squabble is not rare in church history, and it usually emerges whenever the issue of spiritual renewal arises. It boiled over when the Protestant Reformers insisted that beliefs without the gift of faith are worthless, using as a corrective Paul's emphasis on faith alone. Catholics heard this emphasis as talking about belief alone, so they raised the argument that doing needs to be an ingredient in the process. One side was fearful of self-salvation; the other was anxious over the laziness of cheap grace.

Interestingly, it is Paul himself who provides a clue as to how both sides can be right, expressing this tension as a paradox. "Work out your own salvation with fear and trembling," Paul writes, and the Catholics applaud (Phil. 2:12, RSV). But Paul continues: "For God is at work in you, both to will and to work for his good pleasure" (Phil. 2:13, RSV). Cheers arise from the Protestant ranks. But can we have it both ways? Ignatius of Loyola tried by translating this paradox into a livable prescription: "Act as if it all depends upon you; pray as if it all depends on Christ." Paul illustrated with his own life how this paradox is livable. No one worked harder on behalf of Christ than he, likening faith to running a race in order to win the prize (see 1 Cor. 9:24). Yet no one prayed harder than he, resolutely insisting, "It is no longer I who live, but it is Christ who lives in me" (Gal. 2:20).

Let's make this issue concrete. The good news is unbelievably good precisely because we do not deserve it, warrant it, merit it, earn it, or win it. It is a sheer gift. But this is why it is so difficult. One cannot merit a gift but only gasp, "I don't deserve this!" It is easier to give than to receive because we are uncomfortable with receiving anything we do not deserve by earning it. Thus when we do accept a gift, it is usually with the intent to balance the account soon with reciprocity. We dislike feeling indebted to anyone for anything. How rare are those who know how to receive a gift—humbly, gracefully, and thankfully. They can help us realize that in relating to God, it is more blessed to receive than to give; and in dealing with others, it is more blessed to give than to receive. Faith involves this kind of reciprocity.

When the meaning of faith becomes clear, then the function of belief falls into place. Beliefs have little value unless they function to evoke faith by unpacking the rich nuances of living our faith in Christ. Thus grace is the name for faith received as a gift. Pentecost is a name for the experiential integration of faith and belief whereby "your young men shall see visions, and your old men shall dream dreams" (Acts 2:17). Resurrection is a name for life so transformed that death loses its power over us. Annunciation is a name for the divine birthing in Mary that is offered to us as rebirth, adopting us as "joint heirs with Christ" (Rom. 8:17). Incarnation affirms that "God's Spirit dwells in you" and renders our souls temples for the Spirit's residency (1 Cor. 3:16). The kingdom of God on earth points to the new heaven and earth that call us as cocreators to "renew the face of the ground" (Ps. 104:30). Beliefs function as pointers to the richness of faith as lived.

➤ **Has it been true in your own experience that faith is first and belief(s) follow? Are there any central Christian beliefs that you have difficulty using as pointers to an enriched faith?**

Favorite Scriptures

WHY?

Probably each of us has favorite books of the Bible that especially feed us, while others leave us cold. For example, while Matthew is my least favorite Gospel, other persons find it to be their favorite. The explanation that makes the most sense is that each biblical writer has a personal need that provides the orienting focus. Matthew was a tax collector involved in a fraudulent legal system. Understandably, then, his Jesus is primarily a new lawgiver, with clear rules against dishonesty: "Let what you say be simply 'Yes' or 'No'; anything more than this comes from evil" (Matt. 5:37, RSV). Conversion, as Matthew sees it, involves carefully keeping a life record, as God does—one that is accurate, precise, honest, and, above all, accountable. In contrast to his former tax collector colleagues, Matthew insists that one's accounting must "be perfect" (Matt. 5:48).

The approach laid out in the Gospel of Matthew may be coherent and appealing as long as a person inhabits a Matthew-type world. But there are others of us with contrasting needs, and we hope there is a version of the good news for us. Since anxiety over the possibility of abandonment haunts me, I struggle with feelings of worthlessness. Thus my favorite Gospel is Luke, for he focuses on the outcast and the rejected. The Jesus I need is not the one who promises reward for a job well done. I have been a workaholic to a fault, with much of my life consumed in an effort to earn acceptance by proving that I am worth having around. There is no good news for me in hearing that there will be a final life inventory in which heaven depends on whether I've worked hard enough. Such stress would simply escalate my fear of not being found worthy. No, the God I need is not the one who will reward my perfection. The God who has touched my soul is the one portrayed in the parables unique to Luke, exemplifying mercy. The God who embraces me is the father yearning for his wayward son, the widow searching for her lost coin, and the shepherd leaving all behind in search of his abandoned lamb. These parables portray a God who lovingly cares for us. I need understanding not reward, forgiveness not compensation. I need to be embraced not for what I have done or earned, but in spite of my continuing shortcomings.

Which scriptural version touches each of us depends on the primal need that is guiding our individual life's journey. Because of our different needs, the same verses won't resonate with or motivate everyone. Yet, we are all born with some version of neediness, and so we are inevitably motivated by getting. When we begin receiving what we most need from a verse or scripture passage, our attitudes shift toward thankfulness. This transition creates an increasingly serene soul. As we experience this center as firm, our boundaries relax and expand, for we no longer need to clutch the little that we have. Our favorite scripture depends on its particular theme. It may be about how being loved results in becoming loving, or how being welcomed home spawns hospitality, or how being found encourages seeking, or how in being cured one becomes a healer, or how in being forgiven one becomes forgiving. While different scriptures meet different needs, in the end they are all variations on the same theme. We are being fed.

⤳ **Which book of the Bible is your favorite? Which Gospel? Which verse? Why?**

Fearing God

THE YELLING FATHER

Have you ever tripped over a scriptural reference that you had previously skipped over without thought? One particular verse had this effect on me. "You shall fear your God: I am the LORD" (Lev. 19:14). This passage is similar to others, such as when Moses said, "Fear the LORD your God" (Deut. 10:20). Can it really be that our proper posture before God is fear—as in trepidation, dread, even terror? Yet consulting the concordance indicated numerous such declarations. "The fear of the LORD is the beginning of wisdom" (Ps. 111:10). "Come, O children, listen to me. I will teach you the fear of the LORD" (Ps. 34:11).

I likely tripped over this issue today because of the accumulated effect of recent spiritual direction. An obstacle to faith for many persons is the image of God as Father. Recently a friend remarked about this being a barrier for her: "If God is like my father, I am scared of him! It was always his way or not at all." When another person shared his deep fear of God's punishment, I asked him about his father. "What I remember was how he yelled, threatening me because I was never able to please him." In my own childhood, my mother often said, "Wait until your father comes home; he'll put the fear of God in you!"

I still remember how I felt as a child when I turned to the end of the Bible to see how things would turn out. The ending felt like a threat: "I am coming soon!" (Rev. 22:7). With such imagery characterizing our understandings of God, what are we to do when Jesus instructs us to love God with all our hearts, minds, souls, and strength? We often feel a sense of guilt because we cannot love someone whom we fear. With such thoughts running around in my head, I checked the Hebrew and

Greek words that are translated as "fear." To my surprise, I found that they can also be translated as "respect," "reverence," and "standing in awe." Yes! These words clarified the issue. In a real sense, our identity is tied to whomever we hold in awe—be it Babe Ruth, Elvis Presley, or the God revealed in Jesus Christ.

A religion based on fear is worthless. But faith based on awe is another matter. Our Judeo-Christian history can actually be distilled into moments full of awe. We see Israel standing on the far shore of the Red Sea looking back at the event that just liberated them from slavery—that is awe. Exiles singing as they return home from the Babylonian captivity—that is awe. Jesus forgiving his tormentors as they nailed him to the cross—that is awe. Experiencing the incarnate God in the breaking of bread—that is awe. Witnessing the Holy Spirit continuing to transform lives—that too is awesome! By trusting the God revealed in Christ, we find our fears diminished.

➤ **In what ways do you fear God? How might this relate to your relationship with a particular person(s) in your past?**

Forgiveness

A STATE OF BEING

Some Christians insist that without the threat of a hell there would be no incentive for doing good. Yet I find distasteful the thought of heaven populated by persons motivated by saving their own skins. I am reminded of a conversation Jesus had with Peter. Peter asks, probably rhetorically, if forgiving his brother seven times will be sufficient before he has permission to withhold forgiveness. Seventy times seven is Jesus' reply, hoping that before Peter is halfway through counting to 490, he will forget what he is angry about. Jesus understands forgiveness as having less to do with what we are to do as with who we are to be. Forgiving is an orienting attitude, a state of being, a way of life. Thus Jesus' concern is not just for us to forgive but for us to become forgiving. By forgiving 490 times, we practice having a magnanimous disposition.

Although most persons may be open to forgive if the other person expresses genuine sorrow, the Christian disposition is much deeper. Forgiveness is to be extended even to those who do not ask for it, do not believe that they need it, and would likely scorn it even if offered. Such forgiveness is the outward manifestation of love. Yet merely overlooking offenses is not love. Forgiveness motivated by love can be tough, for it involves doing whatever is needed to enable the other person to become loving.

Attaining such an attitude toward others is unlikely unless we have experienced undeserved forgiveness ourselves. The journey to an attitude of loving forgiveness begins with confession as an acknowledgement of our undeserving nature. This first step is the most difficult to take. How many of us with physical symptoms of illness neglect seeing a doctor for fear of learning that we are sick? We refuse to see what our actions look like when seen through the eyes of others for fear of learning that we are guilty. Society provides multiple ways to help us avoid confession. Newspapers are peppered with daily stories of persons getting caught in the wrong, yet the standard response is rarely confession. Instead, the persistent modeling is that of self-justification—making excuses, blaming circumstances, faulting others. And when all else fails, they reluctantly acknowledge having made a mistake. *Sin* is no longer even in our vocabulary. On the national level, the best that an exposed country can be brought to do is mumble an apology. What an unseemly evasion of courage to escape the confessional three-word triad.: "I did it. I was wrong. Please forgive me."

A nationally known television personality, whose assets top a billion dollars, was caught in a scam for making money illegally on the stock market. A newspaper editorial made well our point: "If only she had confessed that she had done wrong and asked forgiveness, the country would have been more than willing to forgive her—but she wouldn't do it." Until we understand that we are undeserving of forgiveness, we cannot even imagine what an attitude of forgiveness is like. Yet that's what Christianity is all about.

➤ **Remember a time when you sought forgiveness from someone. How did it make you feel? Is there anything for which you are unable to ask forgiveness, even from God?**

Friendship

AS SPIRITUAL DIRECTION

*I*t's too bad that we can't remember the two most triumphant accomplishments of our infancy: standing on our own two feet and taking our first faltering steps. What pride our parents must have felt when right in front of them their own flesh and blood mustered such courage and strength. From then on, our growing entails more of the same—striving for the courage to stand increasingly erect and strikingly imposing, with the hopeful ability to enter a room so that it is we who will be noticed. Yet, deep inside, something of that tremulous little child will always remain. Unsure in new situations, we are tempted to revert to some version of crawling if sufficient attention is not forthcoming. So much of our energy is consumed with appearance, pretending to be who we are not sure we really are, hoping to convince others so we can believe it ourselves.

Such a pretension doesn't work very well, at least not for long. Paint peels, youth fades, and fame fleets. Have any of us not experienced times of feeling like a phony, of play-acting, of realizing that we are fooling no one but ourselves? Have any of us not thought, *If others really knew what goes on inside me, they wouldn't like me?*

Yet, ironically, when we dare to be a bit vulnerable with a friend or two, they seem to find us most likable. So it was with Jesus, that the more vulnerable he became, the more profoundly he revealed the nature of God. And in the humiliation of his death we experience Jesus as most divine. Acquaintances become friends when we begin trusting one another with our inner fears and shared tears. Blessed are we who have such a friend, someone who knows all there is to know about us and still offers an accepting embrace. These friends know us so well that they can sing our songs when we forget the words. This kind of relationship is also what makes a spiritual director a friend.

Friendship, then, becomes a powerful tool for understanding our relationship with God. Perhaps the finest compliment Moses ever received was when God said, "I know you by name" (Exod. 33:17). Jesus is more expansive, as with these final words to his disciples: "You are my friends. . . . I have called you friends" (John 15:14-15). "What a Friend We Have in Jesus" is a popular hymn because it affirms the expansiveness of God's friendship through Christ.

During the Israelites' pilgrimage in the Hebrew scriptures, God's desire for a relationship with them intensifies and reveals feelings of hurt, anger, passion, disappointments, and even jealousy. This is the same God who in the New Testament plunges into a friendship with humanity, becoming the incarnate Emmanuel, "God with us." Jesus represents God's vulnerability in human form.

➤ **Name friends with whom you have been or could be vulnerable. How does such intimacy deepen your understanding of God as a vulnerable friend?**

Giveaway

MARBLES AND ALL

When I was quite young I began collecting marbles. I foraged the gutters and playgrounds for them. I kept adding to my treasure, intent on filling a pickle jar. Once accomplished, I would periodically count them, making sure that all the marbles were there. There were ninety-nine of them. My friends enjoyed playing marbles during recess—drawing a circle in the dirt, each person putting in an equal number of marbles, and taking turns trying to knock marbles out of the circle with a shooter. I refused to play marbles "for keeps," unwilling to risk losing even one of my precious ninety-nine. One day I accidentally spilled my marbles, and they rolled everywhere, some even under the furniture. Like the biblical shepherd, I feverishly left those remaining in the jar and sought out the lost. Looking back now, I realize that I didn't have a jar of marbles; in a strange way, the jar had me.

Years later, after my father's funeral, I was tasked with sorting through the accumulated possessions in the old homestead. And there it was—my jar of marbles—in the back of a closet. Unable to resist, I started counting them, laughing out loud when I reached ninety-nine. They were all there. I heard some children playing outside. Hardly realizing what I was doing, I joined them. "How would you kids like some marbles?"

I left behind a host of smiles, an empty pickle jar, a fine sense of freedom, and a hunch that the heart of the gospel resided close by.

⇢ **Which of your possessions are inclined to possess you? Can you give them away?**

Holy Communion

AT THE KITCHEN TABLE

Christians like to eat—potluck gatherings, coffee and donuts between church services, and dinners after funerals. In fact, eating and drinking have always been a part of the Christian life. Beginning with the Last Supper, whenever and wherever Christians gather, they eat and drink.

The Hebrew scriptures provide analogies, such as when Queen Jezebel gives Elijah twenty-four hours to get out of town. Running for his life, Elijah finally falls to the ground, panting for God to "take away [his] life" (1 Kings 19:4). He is too exhausted to go on yet too frightened to stop. God replies, "Get up and eat, otherwise the journey will be too much for you" (19:7). So Elijah eats, and the food sustains him for "forty days and forty nights" (19:8). Forty—the number of years Israel survived in the desert with manna and water from the rock. It is also the number of desert days Jesus was fed by angels. Where can we find such lasting food and drink? We find the answer in the New Testament when Jesus, comparing himself to manna, says, "I am the bread of life" (John 6:48). Thus, he continues, "unless you eat the flesh of the Son of Man and drink his blood, you have no life in you . . . for my flesh is true food, and my blood is true drink" (John 6:53, 55).

Significantly, a sizable portion of each Gospel deals with Jesus' final days, especially the Last Supper. There in the upper room, Jesus instituted the church as his body and prayed that "they may all be one. As you, Father, are in me and I am in you, may they also be in us" (John 17:21). Yet, ironically, it is the Eucharist that has fragmented the church and divided it so that we refuse to eat and drink with our brothers and sisters in Christ.

Much of this fracturing has resulted from our being so preoccupied with how we understand and administer the Body of Christ that we squander the what of the event. An analogy from the Appalachian coal-mining town of my birth has helped me find a path through the disagreements over Eucharist. In my hometown, living rooms are rarely used. Instead, they are reserved for special occasions like weddings, funerals, or visits by the preacher. The real living occurs in the kitchen. Friends never use the front door but always go around to the back. The dented coffeepot is steaming on the coal stove and freshly baked bread and cups with broken handles are on the table. It is here that deep sharing happens. Here the real funerals occur, when over coffee we share stories about the one whose cup is now empty.

The early church, as they endeavored to live out their new understanding of God, reminds me of these kitchen gatherings. The kitchen table, in effect, became the center of worship for the early church. God was no longer a polite parlor guest whose occasional visits were prearranged. The God they experienced in Jesus was so totally one of them, so utterly at home with them, that God used the back door—walking in without knocking, pouring a cup of coffee, and wanting to know the news of the day. This is the God whose real presence they came to know in the breaking of bread and drinking from a handleless cup.

The *how* and *where* can clutter the *what* and *why* of Holy Communion. Thus this simple image of an upper-room kitchen is helpful, in which, surrounded by the aroma of homemade bread, we tell Jesus stories, with our eucharistic prayer emerging from shared laughing, crying, and dreaming. Paul spoke of the Spirit dwelling within the temple of our souls, yet I find the Spirit in a more modest place—at the kitchen table of the heart.

➤ **Identify a few of the times and events in your life that have or could have a eucharistic flavor.**

Home Free

TO SEEK AND TO BE SOUGHT

Perhaps you are envious of persons with whom God always seems present and available—like a smiling shadow or a warm embrace. But for folks like me, God's favorite activity seems to be hide-and-seek.

The Gospel of John relates an episode in which Jesus "hid himself and went out of the temple" (8:59). I think this was a pattern with Jesus. In his home of Nazareth, he so offended folks that they took him to the edge of a cliff, intent on pushing him to his death. But strangely, "he passed through the midst of them and went on his way" (Luke 4:30). Jesus had a knack for being unseen, and he would often disappear up into the hills—his favorite place for playing his version of hide-and-seek. The disciples would have to search for him. They said, "Everyone is searching for you" (Mark 1:37). But Jesus replied, "Let us go on to the neighboring towns" (1:38). In the words of Isaiah, "Truly, [he is] a God who hides himself" (45:15).

Often we find ourselves in Thomas's position, doubting with the hope of seeing the scars of a resurrected Jesus. Jesus said to Thomas, "Blessed are those who have not seen and yet have come to believe" (John 20:29). Jesus made clear that our relating to God is not one of sight but one of promise. This is why the theme of covenant is so important—in which the God who is invisible, apparently absent, has made a promise to always seek us. This is what makes the Emmaus story so moving. Two of the disciples are disappointed over Jesus' death. One says, "We had hoped that he was the one to redeem Israel" (Luke 24:21). They are desolate, for Jesus had apparently broken his promise. Because we have all been scarred by promises never fulfilled, the only

God worth seeking is the one who makes promises that will be kept. When Jesus does return, he is in disguise, and we are told that "[the disciples'] eyes were kept from recognizing him" (Luke 24:16). When finally they finally did recognize Jesus, "he vanished from their sight" (24:31).

Perhaps we have God's version of hide-and-seek all wrong. Instead of hiding in order not to be caught, we hide with the hopes of being caught by the God who promises always to come looking for us. I remember painfully the evening when as a child I hid too well. It started to get dark, and as I huddled in my clever hiding spot, I began to feel alone and scared. Finally I came out of hiding, racing triumphantly toward home base to shout my victory. Instead, I discovered that when my playmates couldn't find me, they just went home. What if this happened with God? By giving up, my friends hadn't played according to the rules. When the one who is searching is unable to find those who are hiding, he is supposed to yell, "Olly olly oxen free."

It has taken me a long time, but finally I think I understand. God continues to search for us until we are all found. Or, God will call, "Olly olly oxen free," letting us know we can come out of our hiding places. The name for God's version of hide-and-seek is *grace*.

⇥ **In what sense is God hidden from you? Is seeking God as important as finding? In what ways do you feel that God is searching for you?**

Humbled

LETTING GO TO BE NOTHING

An abbot preached a deeply moving homily at the funeral of one of his monks, who was both a friend of mine and a famous author and speaker. I was anxious lest the abbot be dishonest about our friend. He was not. The abbot began by acknowledging that our friend had a tendency to be pompous. In the last two years of his life, though, he suffered through "the divinely inspired process of humiliation."

Our friend was shaken by several career disappointments, including a reversal of his lifelong passion to be an abbot. The process humbled him. Against his will, he slowly learned the gospel truth available to each of us when we let go of everything we have ever treasured. The abbot's translation of Jesus' words says it well: "The one who brings himself to nothing will find out who he is"—namely, God's. After a debilitating car accident, our friend experienced loneliness, depression, and, at moments, despair over his indescribable powerlessness. Then one morning, bound to the machines that were keeping him alive, he whispered, "I've had enough."

These are the moments when in being stripped we are open to experiencing the infinite mercy and love of God. Strange though it may seem, we need nothing more. By being nothing, having nothing, and wanting nothing, we abound in everything that matters. Paul put it this way: "Your life is hidden with Christ in God" (Col. 3:3).

➤ **If you were stripped of all your accomplishments, what would be left? Would it be enough?**

Humility

FOR REAL

Virtue is the name given to characteristics of living as Christians. What could rival love on the list of Christian virtues? In my opinion, the answer is humility: "All who exalt themselves will be humbled, and those who humble themselves will be exalted" (Luke 14:11). In the secular world, humility is likely to be considered a weakness. Imagine Jesus being interviewed for the CEO position at a company. The interviewer might ask, "Tell me why we should want to hire you." Jesus would answer, "Because I am humble." I can only imagine this interview would be short. The interviewer might try to explain, "We want someone who is ambitious, forceful, competitive, and driven to be number one!" Surely Jesus wouldn't get the job.

Christian humility is widely misunderstood. It is intended to characterize our relationship with God, not meaning self-humiliation in relating to others. Christian humility involves neither self-defacement nor demeaning subservience. It isn't thinking less of one's self but thinking of one's self less. This is why imparting spiritual direction to persons with undue low self-esteem is difficult. They are not really humble about themselves but obsessed with themselves, fixated on how others see them. Thus they are incapable of accepting themselves as humble unless that would cause persons to treat them as if they were the desired persons they know themselves not to be. The heart of their lament is that they are not the center of anything for anyone.

Low self-esteem, therefore, is simply an exaggerated form of the self-obsession operating in us all. This is why spiritual direction circulates around one reality: that we are created with the profound need to be loved so that we can love. For, as the writer of 1 John reminds us, "whoever does not love abides in death" (3:14). Our dilemma is that the more we struggle to get love by portraying ourselves as lovable, the more our neediness becomes exposed in awkward weakness. Hiding our emptiness in a dissonance of chatter, preoccupied with appearance, we are inclined to posture our insignificance with a flourish. The obsessiveness with receiving clogs our capacity to give, establishing a vicious circle in which we can never truly give or receive.

Humility is the clarifying mark of our significance. The love for which we are created cannot be a self-project, but rather acquired only through relationship. Our significance thus depends on whom we permit to define our significance. If it is our competitive society, then any perceived worth will be temporary and fragile. But being humble before God means granting to God alone the right to determine our significance. It is seeing ourselves through the loving eyes of Christ that gifts us with the courage of indifference to human measurements of significance. "Humble yourselves before the Lord, and he will exalt you" (James 4:10). Released from an obsession with self, we are freed from the need for self-assertion—from seeking attention, from needing recognition, from fixating on what others may be saying or thinking or doing. How others see me or what they may be accomplishing is no longer any of my business.

Jesus had a litmus test for humility—the ability to help those who cannot help us in return. Humility is the firm awareness that standing before God we are all helpless; yet God has "prepare[d] a table before me" so that "my cup overflows" (Ps. 23:5). When loved by God, our low self-esteem may be replaced by a true humility.

➤ **How can you exchange low self-esteem for the kind of humility that encourages you to serve others? Do you want to?**

Imaginative Seeing

THE BEAUTY OF FAITH

Recently I took a friend to an eye doctor for laser surgery. Normally taciturn, all the way home he was unrestrained in expressing his feelings. "Look at that! Do you see that?" With new eyes he was insistent about the greenness of the grass, the blueness of the sky, even the yellowness of McDonald's signs. "I can see!" he exclaimed. "I really can!"

Much of Jesus' healing had to do with the blindness and deafness characterizing our human condition. Jesus said, "Do you have eyes, and fail to see? Do you have ears, and fail to hear?" (Mark 8:18). Paul's conversion occurred when "something like scales fell from his eyes" (Acts 9:18). All of us look at the world through badly scratched and damaged lenses. Contorted by anger, guilt, depression, resentment, frustration, jealousy, and defensiveness, we look but do not see, hear but do not listen. Jesus' ministry involved blinding those who thought they could see and granting sight to those who acknowledged they were blind.

With solid reason, then, the church through the centuries has been a vital patron of the arts—architecture, music, painting, and poetry. The human spirit is stretched toward wholeness in the awesome immensity of a Gothic cathedral, its walls adorned with a Rubens canvas, fronted by a Sutherland tapestry, and incensed with a Fauré requiem. Such baptism into beauty can happen as well in the sacred simplicity of a white clapboard church, its Shaker-like furnishings straight from a Wyeth painting.

Yet many of use live in houses with imitation siding and plastic-covered furnishings. Understandably, the poetry of faith continues to atrophy. More than ever, the gate is narrow, as secular eyes leave us little more than a crack in the wall. Even so, it is wide enough for us spiritual Alices to fall into Christianity's poetic wonderland—where at sunrise birds sing to their Creator, lakes ripple to the touch of angels, clouds are the wind-driven chariots of God, sun and moon rise and set as eucharistic hosts, and steaming coffee on a frosty morning is a chalice toasting the Divine-human marriage feast. Blindness to this daily uncommonness, T. S. Eliot insists, is because of "the door we never opened into the rose-garden." By refusing to be impounded by our culture, the Christian's imagination is unwrapped by the Holy Spirit, drinking from the mysterious interiority of everything, evoked by the hints that the arts provide. Once we are opened to see the beauty of this earth as Jesus did, then each speck within it is beheld as sacred and precious, drawing us into treating creation and every person and part within it as deserving of loving gentleness. Let us pray with Ezra that God "may brighten our eyes" (9:8). To behold a world rich with the vibrancy of God is to exclaim, "I can see!"

➤ **Where do you go and what do you do to have your senses recharged?**

Leaving Your Mark

WITHOUT A TRACE

None of us wants to be forgotten—ever. A recent advertisement offered a cardboard-based, biodegradable casket that will decompose at the same rate as the human body. This product might appeal to the ecologically inclined, but I have a hunch that most persons will find the heavy metal casket—sealed in a waterproof vault and complete with a refundable guarantee that it will defy all of nature's onslaughts—more appealing. The biodegradable casket flies in the face of a deep and often nasty human motivation—to leave one's mark one way or another.

I found my visit to Stonehenge to be disappointing, mainly because of the barbed-wire fence that kept me at a distance. A guard explained the need for it: "It is an unfortunate necessity to keep visitors from desecrating these cherished rocks by carving their names." Leaving our mark is a temptation that we widely execute, even to despoiling prehistoric cave paintings, irreplaceable redwood trees, and other natural wonders. Abandoned buildings, railroad cars, stadium seats, interstate overpasses—all are fair game for this human obsession. Even an acclaimed astronaut announced with pride that he had left his footprint on the moon.

Such actions defy the words accompanying our Ash Wednesday service: "From dust you come and to dust you shall return." Some folks find these words ominous, but in expressing clearly our lives' status, they provide an important humbling. We are earth's reverent guests, never its owners. There is something nasty about cutting the earth into discrete pieces and selling them off, notarizing deeds in pretense that our ownership is everlasting. Contrary to this human propensity to grasp, clutch, own, and mark everything we touch, scripture ascribes us to roles as gentle stewards of God's earth. Evidence of our fallenness is this twisted allure to trash the world as proof of our existence.

God's gift to us is a soul that yearns for Eden. When we begin to see the earth as not our own, Eden reappears everywhere—and God invites us to accompany the One who walks "in the garden in the cool of the day" (Gen. 3:8, NKJV).

⤞ **On what have you left your mark? On whom? How does the knowledge that you will return to ashes connect you with God's creation?**

Letting Go

OF THE UNFORGIVEABLE

Forgiveness is not easy. Initially, we might suspect that it is easier to receive forgiveness than to offer it. Yet this may not be the case, for accepting forgiveness entails acknowledging guilt, humbling us by accepting a gift we have neither earned nor deserve.

Offering forgiveness to those who are apparently unaware of having hurt us can also be difficult. Often in spiritual direction I hear these words: "I know my father must have loved me, but he never told me." These persons do not know that they were loved, and in never having heard the words, serious doubt continues to cripple them. Ironically, many parents seem oblivious to the hurt they have caused, would be defensive if told, and would be bewildered, if not offended, by being offered forgiveness. Time rarely heals such a condition, condemning us to a treadmill of rehearsed hurting. In pulling at the scabs and massaging the bruises, past hurts become present wounds that never seem to heal.

Whether these past hurts are of the emotional, psychological, and/or physical variety; and whether inflicted by commission, omission, or as collateral damage, few of us escape unharmed. Yet many believe that their only option for healing is to forget past hurts that may never be acknowledged by those who caused the hurting. But forgetting is not a viable option, even if the offending person is dead. Unless we find some release from our bruised pasts, we will continue to carry those burdens. Damaging words to a vulnerable child take residency at soul depth, re-echoing down the corridors of memory until they become regarded as a self-assessment. Those who hear, "You can't do anything right!" can ultimately conclude, "I am incompetent!" Even small mistakes serve as proof that the whispering voice inside your head is accurate, becoming self-fulfilling prophecies. In trying to protect yourself from further injury, you do to others what you fear they might do to you.

Is there freedom from such entrapment? By identifying the originating voice or voices, we come to realize that what that person said or did is not our responsibility, but permitting that hurt to continue to stain and define us now is. I become my own enemy when I perpetuate the hurt that deserves a definitive burial. Without forgiveness, such hurts can last a lifetime. If viewed from the perspective of self-interest, not to forgive is masochism. Rehearsing past bruises is like keeping a rusty nail within your heart, a worm in your mind, a disease in your soul. Holding on to resentment is like drinking poison and waiting for your enemy to suffer and die. Not to forgive is to give the owner of the past voices or acts the power to keep wounding me now. Jesus' dictum to love one's enemy is a prescription for healing.

After identifying the voices comes the hard part—taking the first step in forgiving the undeserving. Here we need to hear from the letter to the Romans that "God proves his love for us in that while we still were sinners Christ died for us" (5:8). Undeserving of forgiveness, God takes the first step that us washes clean. God takes the initiative with us always—even before we have a clue that we need forgiveness. So if Christ pays the price, picks up the tab, takes the hit, and declares himself guilty, then we are stripped of every reason to restrict our forgiveness to those who deserve it, ask for it, or even want it. Forgiving those who have hurt us—what unparalleled peace.

➤ **Whose voice inside you still has the most power to haunt? Are you willing to forgive in order to be free?**

Martyrdom

COLOR-CODED

Let's take a look at Saint Bernard's proposal of color-coding martyrs—red, green, and white. The red ones are the gory kind, those who die violent deaths for Christ. Oscar Romero is a recent example, slain as he presided at the Eucharist for siding with the poor. The green variety are martyrs of struggling conscience—those who might prefer to be red martyrs but instead spread their martyrdom over a lifetime. Athanasius would nominate Saint Anthony as one of these, living a long life plagued by horrendous conflicts of inner desires. Paul understood green martyrdom: "I delight in the law of God in my inmost self, but I see in my members another law at war. . . . Who will rescue me from this body of death?" (Rom. 7:22-24).

Red martyrdom is likely to be quick, horrific, and sudden. The green variety is usually quiet, long, and internal, until some event commands witness. Martyrdom of the white variety is more available to the rest of us. It is hidden and ordinary, stretched out daily for a long and tedious segment of one's life. "Keeping on keeping on" expresses a white martyr's outer appearance, while inwardly such a life feels unglamorous, like any ordinary person doing ordinary things. Characterized by an intentional mindfulness, white martyrs refuse personal and societal distractions and deceptions. Persevering in the headlight glare of death's inevitability, they love boldly in the face of whatever loss, betrayal, or abandonment may befall, living quietly and with steadfast constancy their pangs of doubt. This lifestyle is lived for its own sake, freed from desire for reward or fear of punishment. Paul describes it paradoxically "as having nothing, and yet possessing everything" (2 Cor. 6:10). A white martyr's reward, said Gregory the Great with a touch of envy, is a profound inner peace untainted by even a desire for outward approval, willing to live unnoticed and ignored, their martyrdom so hidden that it is ineligible for applause.

Acknowledging that red and green martyrs will always be a decided minority, Paul calls every Christian a saint in expectation that we will trudge the white path. Jesus calls it picking up one's cross and following him. The old hymn asks rhetorically if Jesus "must bear the cross alone." No. "There's a cross for everyone."

➤ **Are there any situations in which you could imagine yourself willing to sacrifice your life? To what degree would it be a decision of faith?**

Memories

ACHING TO BE REDEEMED

In providing spiritual direction, I find that the struggles many persons have are rooted in childhood memories, some actively remembered and some repressed. Recently, someone working on his spiritual direction experienced an important breakthrough: he stumbled upon the repressed memory of his fifth birthday. He remembered that this birthday was to mark his coming of age—he was a kindergarten student who would enter first grade in the fall. The day finally arrived. He waited for someone to acknowledge his special day. But the time for bed came and went and nothing. The man broke into sobbing just thinking about what happened. "They totally forgot!" he exclaimed. We explored together how this event shaped his world then—and how it shapes it even now. Love denied folds back upon itself.

I never seemed able to please my mother, providing a tension that was operative as far back as I can remember. Some years after she died, I found myself unable to move beyond the fourth station while doing the stations of the cross. In the fourth station, Jesus encounters his mother while carrying the cross. I stood there, slowly drawn into being Jesus, sweating profusely under the weight of the cross, looking up expecting to hear her reprimand: "Paul, comb your hair. What will the neighbors think?" Although my mother was physically dead, that moment I realized how very alive she was within me. I also realized how unhealthy it would be to avoid much longer the confrontation that might bring closure. The lid had been pried open on a host of repressed childhood memories, and the struggle was now current, painful, and graphic, but I felt a sense of urgency to move forward.

Eventually I was ready to confront my relationship with my mother. At her grave, I spoke: "Mom, I think I understand now. All that you ever wanted was to hear your father say, 'I love you, Ruth.' He never did, even though you tried by being an incredibly obedient daughter. So you attempted to raise me to be his perfect grandchild so that he would love you for being the perfect mother. That didn't work either. He could not tell you what you needed to hear because he never heard those words from his mother. Mom, all you needed to hear from him was all that I needed to hear from you. I understand now why it couldn't be said. May God forgive us all. We tried. Mom, I love you."

Healing often requires revisiting our childhood deprivations and hurts. Our original traumas were intense because we were all alone—small, fragile, and vulnerable. But this time, perhaps with a spiritual director, the healing visitation of our primal hurts is done mindfully with Jesus as a strengthening presence. Jesus is the one who lovingly beckons the children to him, especially those who know what it is like to cry alone in the night. We are no longer alone.

➵ **Which of your childhood memories need this kind of revisiting? Are you willing to visit them with someone—Jesus, a friend, a spiritual director—by your side?**

Miracles

WHAT TO DO WITH THEM

Wouldn't believing be a lot easier if our faith story weren't so intertwined with miracles? For Jews, the bottom line is the Red Sea miracle—when God's chosen people were delivered from slavery for new life in a promised land. For Christians, the Resurrection delivered us from sin and death into a promise of a new heaven and a new earth. For many years I craved seeing a miracle, a teeny one, right there in front of me—just enough to temper my doubts and counter my uncertainties. The disciple Thomas understood. He said, "Unless I see the mark of the nails in his hands . . ." (John 20:25). But while he got his miracle by putting his finger in the nail holes, I haven't.

It helped to realize that persons can be exposed to miracles and never see them. Even participation in a miracle requires faith. Take the Israelites at the Red Sea. Moses was a smart strategist, carefully planning Israel's escape route. He intentionally camped Israel with their back to the shallow water that scholars identify as the Sea of Reeds. By appearing to be foolishly vulnerable, Moses lured Pharaoh into thinking that his army would capture the defenseless runaways. Then, as scripture describes it, "the LORD drove the sea back by a strong east wind all night, and turned the sea into dry land" (Exod. 14:21)—and under the cover of darkness, with the gale muffling their movement, Moses led his people across. Seeing what was happening, the shocked Egyptians plunged in, but God "clogged their chariot wheels so that they turned with difficulty" (14:25). In the ensuing panic, Israel's escape was assured. Moses and the Israelites proceeded to call out to God in thanksgiving. Miracle or coincidence, God or luck—either interpretation involves wagering.

As T. S. Eliot might inform the skeptics, you "had the experience but missed the meaning."

In Tornado Alley where I live, common are the curious reports of persons and buildings miraculously saved. We hear reports of other supposed miracles as well, but what difference does it make? The primal miracles for Jews and Christians are less about breaking natural law and more about the transformed lives of those who believe in them. What matters about these events of liberation and resurrection is their power to call forth persons for the work of liberation and resurrection. For those who believe but do not do, the miracle is no longer miraculous.

The meaning of the Red Sea event resides in the desert living of those for whom the Promised Land hope tints the horizon of their imaginations. Resurrection means our old selves are crucified with Christ so that our new selves may arise from the dead. In the end, the real miracle is faith as a gift. The ability to believe with all one's heart, mind, soul, and strength—now that is miraculous.

➤ **How do you compare the miracles from the Bible to the "miracles" in your own life?**

Ordinariness

AS EXTRAORDINARY

The church calendar confirms what many of us feel—the largest portion of our time is just ordinary time. But what is ordinary really like? Maybe it's like having your kids with their kids leave after spending a week with you. Ah, returning to the ordinary. Perhaps it's like coming home after work, kicking off your shoes, falling asleep in front of the TV, and in due time being awakened for supper. Ah, delightfully ordinary. Or maybe it means changing into old clothes and getting dirty in the garden.

We actually find it difficult to be ordinary—because we don't want to be just ordinary. Much of our lives are spent hiding our ordinariness by impressing teachers, bucking for promotions, getting degrees, dressing so as to be noticed, trying to be the witty center of attention. Many persons who come for spiritual direction identify anxiety as their reason for seeking help. When pressed, the root of the problem is often an obsession with Jesus' question to his disciples, but focused on themselves—"Who do people say that I am?" (Mark 8:27). Our difficulties begin when we permit our identities to be defined and thus determined by others. As a result, we become obsessed with pretending to be who we believe others would like us to be. Thus, appearance becomes identity. Anxiety is the mark of not knowing—and fearing to know—who we really are.

The way out begins by asking again the question that started us down the wrong road, but this time of a different person: "Lord, who do you say I am?" How frightening it is to have our masks of extraordinariness pulled off. We find ourselves nakedly and painfully ordinary—

dull, monotonous, tedious, dreary, and tiresome. Who on earth wants to risk knowing what we have spent much of our lives hiding? It's far safer to "see in a mirror, dimly," than "face to face" (1 Cor. 13:12). We fear the day when we shall "know fully, even as [we] have been fully known" (13:12).

Yet conversion happens the day we dare to ask Christ who we are. Braced for the worst, his response is astonishing: "You are the lamb who wandered off, the one I left all the other sheep to find." Really? "You are the lost coin for whom I turned the whole house upside down." You're kidding! "It was for you that I gave my life." Suddenly, whatever anyone else thinks of me is insignificant. I feel the wonderful freedom of being ordinary, no longer needing to pretend otherwise. What a difference it makes to know as we are known by Christ, for in his eyes to be ordinary is to be quite extraordinary.

➷ **Whose opinion of you gets in the way of accepting yourself in the way Jesus sees you?**

Peace

AS HERESY

*I*n recent elections, many heralded Christianity as the custodian of family values. This is true, but in a far deeper sense than declaring the church to be protector of society's version of a nuclear family. Christian living is grounded on the premise that God creates all humanity to be one family, permitting no exclusion, not even enemies. "I bow my knees before the Father," writes Paul, "from whom every family in heaven and on earth takes its name" (Eph. 3:14-15). Theologians regard the Trinity as our cosmic model, revealing the heart of God to be profoundly social, using the analogy of family to understand the relationship of Father, Son, and Holy Spirit.

How, then, are we to understand Jesus' assertion that he came to splinter families—bringing not "peace to the earth" but division, pitting "father against son and son against father, mother against daughter and daughter against mother" (Luke 12:51, 53)? The meaning, I believe, is that since one universal human family is God's goal for history, peace can be a Christian heresy. The predominant motive behind the peace advocated by powerful nations and individuals is to preserve their advantage within an unjust status quo. The condition of our world is such that to preserve the way things are now is to guarantee inequality of all sorts. The *haves* are those who gain most from peace. The powerful nations arm themselves to supposedly maintain the peace so that the *have-nots* will be kept from gaining the equality that is indispensable for a genuine human family. Today's world is a very dysfunctional family.

Maintaining peace in today's unjust world, then, is the way of vetoing change. Two-thirds of the world's population lives in poverty, while privileged nations mount enormous military budgets. The three wealthiest countries in the world have more assets than the combined wealth of the forty-eight poorest countries. When we react to this injustice, our restlessness is labeled subversive, evoking immediately either overt or covert "peacekeeping." The biblical writers expose this predicament by insisting that "righteousness and peace will kiss" only if righteousness marches first and prepares the way for peace (Ps. 85:10). Righteousness and justice bring peace, while peace without them is sin.

Thus the Prince of Peace knows that when we his followers insist on justice coming first, we will cause division with those whose advantage it is to insist upon peace being first. Jesus sides unabashedly with the *have-nots*—the poor, the disdained, and the unwanted—and in so doing exposes the hypocrisy of the *haves*. "Woe to you who are rich, for you have received your consolation," proclaimed Jesus (Luke 6:24). Whether the focus is on nation, class, gender, or individual, the author of the book of James sounds the warning: "Come now, you rich people, weep and wail for the miseries that are coming to you" (5:1).

Jesus knows full well that following him will mean being hated by those who profit from the way things are politically, economically, religiously, and culturally. The case of Paul and Silas is to the point. Wherever they went, the authorities reported that "these people who have been turning the world upside down have come here also" (Acts 17:6). Jesus is consistent. Resurrection is on the far side of the cross; peace is on the far side of justice. To desire peace is to work for justice.

➵ **How would this sequence of justice then peace make a difference in your personal actions? your use of resources? the priorities of your local church?**

Playful Work

OBSERVING THE SABBATH

A nasty tendency that we Christians have is to take a teaching meant to be freeing and turn it into a burden. As a child, I experienced this problem as it related to the third commandment: "Remember the sabbath day, and keep it holy" (Exod. 20:8). As my parents understood it, Sunday meant no cooked meals, no shopping, no work, and certainly no playing. If a button popped off my pants, its repair would wait until Monday because, as Mother insisted, "any sewing done on Sunday will have to be taken out with your nose in heaven." My father's professional baseball career ended abruptly when his contract required that he play baseball on Sundays. My own piety was sorely tested the day my Sunday school teacher likened heaven to a perpetual Sunday.

According to my parents' ethic, the more I relinquished what I wanted to do and have, the better Christian I would be. I know now that some things I was taught as ends were intended to be means. Forbidding sabbath work was for the sake of liberating workaholics like me. Even God took a leisurely seventh day to enjoy creation for its own sake. My parents had it backwards. The restriction on not working on the sabbath was aimed straight at me—giving me license to go play. Play is the name for whatever one does for the joy of it. This is why God insisted that Moses balance Israel's time of work and celebration by scheduling feast days to make merry.

Once we sense a need for balance, the distinction between work and play becomes refreshingly vague and marvelously flexible. What constitutes work has less to do with what is done than with the attitude brought to the doing. For example, I love working with wood, and often a project will extend late into the night. I stop only when I've become exhausted in my playing. Christians are given a weekly sabbath in order to experience a lost Eden as a foretaste of a promised kingdom. In this way, we are fashioned in the image of the Creator God as playful cocreators in gardening the creation toward completion.

⇥ **Set aside some weekend time to do something playful that you fondly remember doing as a child. How might taking time for play improve your attitude about work?**

Prayer

SO SIMPLE

I am constantly surprised by how little Christians know about prayer. Often people may know only, "Now I lay me down to sleep." Many of those seeking spiritual direction often cite a desire to learn to pray. Prayers of all kinds permeate scripture—thanksgiving for victories, confessing of sins, asking for forgiveness, wondering at the beauty of creation, bemoaning God's silence, and supplicating for others. Many books on prayer mistakenly give the impression that prayer is complex, making it feel inaccessible to the average Christian. Abstract language tends to be used, with steps and stages and ladders and types that tend to confuse and frustrate. As I heard one person grumble, "I don't want an advanced course in being a saint; I just need help getting started!"

While prayers vary, praying itself is not complicated. Since prayer is about a relationship with God, our own earthly friendships provide an analogy. When we are with a friend, we talk, finding joy simply in sharing our thoughts, our lives, and ourselves. Some may wonder if God really wants to hear about all the mundane portions of our lives. I contend that the issue is not what is shared but the sharing itself, no matter how inane its content. Prayer at its heart is chattering with God, keeping company for its own sake. As with good friends, all emotions are included and welcomed.

Brother Lawrence, the French lay brother of a Carmelite monastery in the 1600s, applied this understanding of prayer to his daily duties as a monastic cook. God was quaintly his cooking companion. Brother Lawrence included God in everything—from asking God's opinion about spicing the soup to sharing the aroma of lilacs outside the kitchen window. Experiencing the presence of God this way is like spending time with a dear friend. It is interesting that we become embarrassed if someone hears us talking to ourselves, yet we speak internally to ourselves all the time. Therefore, by building upon this trait, praying without ceasing becomes an ongoing conversation with God—instead of ourselves—in which everything is shared: opinions, thoughts, feelings, dilemmas, and problems.

Now let's take our analogy one step further. Picture a mature couple sitting together. On some evenings they may say very little. They don't need to—for their intimacy has become so deep that they already know each other's thoughts and feelings, and they are content simply to be quietly together. In this sense, we see prayer not as conversation but as contemplation. By employing the latter, we lose ourselves in God, in a presence beyond words, for there is no need to ask or to want anything beyond the relationship for its own sake.

By comparing our practices of prayer to God with our friendships, we can choose to pray through conversation or by presence. All talk of types and methods is basically elaborations on these two methods. The hard part, then, is not understanding prayer but the discipline of making prayer a way of life. To achieve this, set aside regular periods of time to cultivate a friendship with God.

➔ **Practice these two methods of prayer with the goal of transitioning from merely saying prayers to leading a prayerful life.**

Rebuffed

WITH A BLUEBERRY HAT

Offering gifts to others involves risk. A painful memory for me began high in the Appalachian Mountains after a week of attending a Boy Scout camp. As we waited to be driven home, I remembered a field of wild blueberries that I had seen on the far side of a hill. I picked a handful to taste, and they were delightful, sufficient to suggest that an hour of picking would make a fine gift for my mother to make a pie. Hot and sweaty, I persevered, filling my wide-brimmed Boy Scout hat.

I carefully held my gift all the way home. When I got to my house, I found my mother reading. I proudly exclaimed, "Look what I brought for you!"

She responded harshly, "What am I supposed to do with these?" When I mumbled something about a pie, she continued to speak about how I was always creating more work for her. She returned to her book, and I carried my berry gift out to the backyard. They didn't taste very good anymore, and I threw them out.

I still have that hat with the blueberry stains. This memory taught me and continues to teach me about the God whom the prophets portray—the God who yearns to bestow gifts and blessings upon us. Scripture uses various imagery to describe our responses to God's gracious gifts—marriage to a faithless spouse or being heartbroken by a former love. But above all, God wants us to know what it is like to have God's tokens of love rebuffed. God showers us with gifts, many times never even receiving a thank-you. We can see this in the book of Hosea, wherein God cries out in anger, "My people are bent on turning away from me." (11:7). God is the one who cuddled and healed Israel when

she was a child, only to be rejected. But with tears of love God continues, "How can I give you up . . . ?" (11:8). After reading this, I realized
that God too has a blueberry hat.

❥ **Recall a time when you experienced a "blueberry hat" moment.
How did it make you feel? What did the experience teach you
about God and gratitude?**

Rejection

BEING A LEPER

All of us, in our own ways, are lepers. Luckily for us, lepers have always been especially dear to Jesus. He is the only person not terror-stricken by the possibility of catching leprosy. Moses exiled lepers, forcing them to wear bells and call out to warn others that they should not be approached or touched for they were unclean. Lepers may lose feeling in their limbs but not in their souls. How excruciating to be an outcast, unfit for any human contact. But while physical leprosy is less prevalent today, spiritual leprosy is at an all-time high. Teenagers who are perceived as different can be ostracized and bullied. As adults, we treat one another no better; we inflict pain with a cutting word, a dirty look, an offhand judgmental remark, or by ignoring those who are unlike us. This exclusion by others renders us spiritual lepers.

Ironically, such hurtful and exclusionary behavior is actually rooted in our deep yearning for belonging and acceptance. When we are deprived of these feelings, we compensate by excluding others. This spiritual leprosy is contagious, and we spread it by modeling it to others or by evoking an analogous defensiveness in them. Spiritual direction often uncovers spiritual leprosy, and I find that it usually has originated quite early in a person's life—when he or she was not touched, held, or affirmed in the moments when it was most needed.

In the Gospel of Mark, we see Jesus encounter a leper in a way that is symbolic of his entire ministry. A leper comes to Jesus to ask for healing. This act is utterly forbidden, and the leper displayed great courage and trust in believing that Jesus will not reject him. Jesus rewards the leper's act of faith by touching him and making him clean.

After offering healing, Jesus sends the former leper back into the very city that has exiled him as a witness that no one is beyond Jesus' healing. But Jesus remains with the outcasts. Every society forces some folks to exist outside the city walls as lepers—in ghettos, reservations, and prisons. Jesus chooses to live in these places. He was born outside in a stable and was crucified with criminals. Jesus knew firsthand what it meant to be a spiritual leper—an outcast among outcasts, rejected, bruised, and heartbroken. As was written in Isaiah, "He was despised and rejected by others" (53:3).

Jesus offers three words to the lepers everywhere: *I love you.* Sometimes these are the only words we need to hear. When we live into Jesus' acceptance of us, we become impervious to what others can do to us, for now "nothing will hurt you" (Luke 10:19). Therefore, "when reviled, we bless; when persecuted, we endure; when slandered, we speak kindly" (1 Cor. 4:12-13).

➤ **Name persons who have made you feel like a leper. Name persons whom you have made to feel that way. Do you make yourself feel like a leper? How can Jesus' love change this?**

Relationships

BROKEN AND RECONCILED

Spiritual direction often involves helping a person reconcile with someone else. Yet in moments of forgiveness, I have often heard, "Okay, I'll forgive him—but I won't forget!" Never forgetting what persons have done against us makes us hostages of our own memories. In so doing, we punish not only others but also ourselves. A minister friend refused a janitorial position to a former parishioner recently released from jail. The minister's reasoning was: "I may forgive him, but he has to live with the consequences of his act." The man's short imprisonment became a life sentence inflicted by those unwilling to give him a second chance.

The gospel perspective is radically different from the "forgive but not forget" mentality. Without exception, we are all guilty of sin. When Jesus told the Pharisees that only those who had not sinned could cast stones, they could not throw even a pebble. If all our wrongs were to be publicly disclosed, none of us could withstand the humiliation. "If you, O LORD, should mark iniquities, Lord, who could stand?" (Ps. 130:3).

I cannot quite imagine what an unblemished innocence would be like, yet I hunger for it. The church offers baptism as a means to make all things new; confirmation is the Spirit's sealing of our commitment to embody it; confession is the vehicle for our ongoing renewal. "If any one is in Christ, he is a new creation; the old has passed away" (2 Cor. 5:17, RSV).

Often we turn our inability to forgive around on ourselves. We might say, "God may have forgiven me, but I cannot forgive myself." Here again is the problem of not being able to forget. We allow the damaging power of the past to remain in the present. Not to surrender such memories to God is to doubt the thoroughness of God's forgiveness. To God, our sins simply no longer exist; they are gone, out of mind, never to be remembered, washed, purged, and wiped away. Our sins are erased from God's memory, and the power of forgiveness is offered both to us the doers and us the receivers.

God's promise of forgiveness can be found throughout scripture. "You have cast all my sins behind your back," insists Isaiah (38:17). Our transgressions are removed "as the east is from the west" (Ps. 103:12). Blessed are we whose "transgression is forgiven, whose sin is covered" (Ps. 32:1). God "will tread our iniquities under foot. [God] will cast all our sins into the depths of the sea" (Mic. 7:19). Incredible? Absolutely.

➵ **What hurt done to you most resists forgetting? What hurt have you caused that remains in your memory? How can trusting God's forgiveness bring forgetting?**

Religion

NOT SPIRITUALITY

A fashionable tendency in today's society is to replace the idea of religion with spirituality. Frequently I hear people say, "I'm not religious, but I am spiritual." For some persons, *religion* has come to mean "churchy" activities, while *spirituality* supposedly refers to a positive inner attitude.

But *religion*, functionally defined, is the name for one's world of meaning. It is the way in which a person makes sense out of life and thus gives purpose to one's living. Thus each of us has a religion. For many folks, however, their religion is unconscious, functioning as a personal version of the competitive individualism fashioned for them by our materialistic society, motivated by a dream of upward mobility. Their interest in spirituality, then, realized or not, is as a coping mechanism for living their religion with less stress and without need to question it.

Thus the church needs to be a bit skeptical about this fad of spirituality, insisting instead on Christianity as a religion that provides a unique way of living. This idea of religion is a lively alternative to the one implicit within our society. The church, by its very presence, has the task of encouraging others to become self-conscious about their functional religion, testing its power to give life authentic meaning. Christianity is a religion and not a spirituality; Christianity is about transforming and not just coping.

⤳ **How is your interest in spirituality affecting positively and/or negatively your attitude toward religion?**

Remembering

AN EXERCISE IN PAIN AND JOY

There comes a point in our lives when we are forced to acknowledge that one or both of our parents can no longer take care of themselves. We may be inclined to insist that our parents leave their homestead for an assisted-living facility, one equipped with medical care as needed. Sometimes a move from home to skilled care works, but often it begins a grieving process in the spirit. Our loved ones tend to shrivel when placed in surroundings no longer baptized by memories and embraced by walls smudged with tears and ceilings the color of recalled laughter.

Spiritual direction with older adults often discloses how such transitioning comes at the price of giving up an important part of their lives. *Incarnation* is the word for how God in Christ becomes totally immersed in all that makes us human. Becoming human occurs as we become incarnate in a world of places and things that give fullness to our lives. Thus, while the world of older adults may look small or confined to some, each one's world is unique, containing experiences etched indelibly on the long-term memory of the soul. Each mark, color, and fixture in their homes has a story aching to be told. A few rotting boards hanging from a branch recalls a treasured tree house. An unruly shrub evokes the presence of a dead spouse who planted it with hope.

I once was certain that the closing of the coal mines of my childhood Appalachian town would render it a ghost town. There were hard times, yet now many folks are moving back to retire in the midst of their memories. Sacred for me are the times when in sharing spiritual direction with older adults they begin to trust me enough to share in turn the yellowing picture albums of their sacred histories. There is joy in these memories but also sadness, for with their deaths, these treasured mementos will, at best, become forgotten in the corner of a relative's attic. And when no one is left to smile knowingly at the faces in a tattered album, a once beloved treasure might become trash. How tragic unless, as the gospel promises, God remembers, always and forever. For our joys and sorrows remain sacred in God's memory. While "senior moments" jostle our short-term memories, our long-term ones have a way of surviving. Christ's incarnation is the assurance that God's long-term memory is in good shape.

➤ **Identify some special memories in your life that are worth never being forgotten. Is your faith able to provide such assurance?**

Resurrection

ARE YOU KIDDING?

Each of us needs an occasional dose of doubt. Spiritual direction has a way of providing it. While studying philosophy, I began to stumble over the concept of the Resurrection. I could no longer conceive that a dead man could be brought back to life. Later, I followed the rabbit trail a little further and became intrigued less with the question, Could it happen? and more with the question, What difference would it make? While some believers concern themselves with the afterlife, my need is to know whether our living counts for anything in the grand scheme of things. Neither Saint Paul nor I want to be "running in vain" (Gal. 2:2).

William Saroyan, in his play *Time of Your Life* proposes that we must live so as to not "add to the misery and sorrow of the world." But not having lived at all would accomplish that! Even as Boy Scouts we learned to leave the campsite better than we found it. Life makes no sense to me if our struggles, joys, sufferings, creativity, sorrows, and even failures are obliterated by death. Unless it matters that each of us has lived, loved, hoped, and dreamed, life is a cruel joke.

In Jesus' teaching about the Last Judgment, I found the promise I needed. We are told that whatever good we have done in the world, "you did it to me" (Matt. 25:40). If our actions are experienced by Christ, they live on forever. When Jacques Maritain and I were teaching at Princeton, we got into an argument. He insisted that the kingdom of God means God will restore the world to how it was in the garden of Eden. But circling everything back to where it began would erase everything that ever happened. Maritain saw his vision as hope. I saw it as a nightmare, rendering the works of our hands to have been done in vain.

Resurrection now had my attention. Remembering the Bible's promise to make "all things new" (Rev. 21:5), Saint Paul saw through the eyes of the resurrected Christ a vision so magnificent that he called the Fall fortunate. My doubts had begun over a puny meaning of resurrection, but then I found myself overwhelmed by a grace-filled culmination of history for which the works of our hands are indispensable. In Nicolas Berdyaev's *The Beginning and the End*, I found my questions deepened: Will our acts have an honorable place in eternal life? Berdyaev's positive answer portrays the kingdom of God not as a linear progress but as progression into God. He believes that Shakespeare's tragedies; the paintings of da Vinci, Rembrandt, and Botticelli; the sculpture of Michelangelo; the symphonies of Beethoven; the writings of Pascal, Tolstoy, Dostoyevsky, and Nietzsche; and the ponderings of Plato, Kant, and Hegel all enter into the kingdom of God. This is true not only for the great acts but even for our smallest achievements.

I know now that resurrection offers the vision worth faith's wager—the works of our hands and the yearnings of our souls are entering even now into the kingdom of God. By living now as if the kingdom yet to be is already present, light is triumphing over darkness, meaning over senselessness, beauty over ugliness, and freedom over necessity.

➻ **Describe the vision of the kingdom of God that your faith provides. How much does it focus on this life? on the next? on you? on others? Is it balanced? big enough? worth dying for?**

Satan

OR THE SATANIC

I wonder if you have the same doubts that I have about Satan—the one popularly pictured with pointed ears, spiked tail, an ominous pitchfork, and a terrible sunburn. Scripture insists that God is an invisible spirit, so it doesn't make sense that God's antagonist should be conceived as a fleshly demon. Yet even with my life swept fairly clear of demons, I find that I cannot disbelieve in the demonic. Even without Satan, I believe firmly in the satanic. There is a power operative in everything that exists, continually defying the creative power of God. Metal rusts, wood rots, rocks crumble, plastic becomes brittle, and life dies.

Not only is the struggle external but also, as Carl Jung identifies, there is a shadow side operating within that expresses itself outwardly. Freud insists that within us a "death wish" is at odds with our "life wish." Is there any one of us who has not gone to bed wishing never to awaken? I confess that the lure of mountain climbing for me contains a fascination with taunting death, and even, in a strange way, being wooed by her. Struggle is all around—hot and cold, dark and light, life and death—everywhere and in everything.

This conflict between being and nonbeing helps us understanding Jesus' ministry with unclean spirits. Modern candidates for demonic status run the gamut of obsessions and addictions—sex, anger, alcohol, gambling, jealousy, pedophilia, drugs, pornography. The one I know best is nicotine. I stopped smoking two decade ago after three decades of nasty self-deception. For the rest of my life I will be resisting this craving, one cigarette away from three packs a day. For years I bought individual packs instead of money-saving cartons because each pack was going to be my last. Insidious are the games we play with ourselves in perpetuating unhealthy behaviors that we know to be contrary to what we claim we want to do and be.

This accounts for the widespread emergence of 12-step programs, no longer countering only "demon rum" but casting out an unbelievable menagerie of unclean spirits. Daily, this healing that Jesus offered is extended to millions, beginning with a confession of powerlessness to cast out one's addiction. The next step is surrendering one's life to a higher power, followed by ongoing confession, forgiveness, and making amends. Members of AA groups are more honest versions of the rest of us, struggling corporately with the process of experiencing the healing that we all need. We should regard them as mirrors in which to recognize our own obsessions. I believe so fully in this process that I am uneasy about trusting any person for whom confession and forgiveness are not a regular practice. This 12-step program is thoroughly Christian, distilling the healing process of Jesus—ongoing surrender, confession, forgiveness, reconciliation, and freedom. Through Christ, "forgiveness of sins is proclaimed to you; by this Jesus everyone who believes is set free" (Acts 13:38-39). *Set free.* The very sound of the words brings a smile to my face and peace to my heart.

⇥ **What in your life could become an obsession or addiction? How might your faith create a countervailing power?**

Self-Love

AS HERESY

Self-help manuals are often tainted by one particular Christian heresy: "You can't love God," we are told, "if you can't love yourself." But this sets before us the incredible task of making ourselves lovable, exacerbating our dilemma in two ways. First, it reinforces our focus on ourselves, which makes us unlikable from the start. Second, such self-help programs treat symptoms, not causes. A major reason why we cannot love ourselves is that we have been loved so little, which forces us into trying to make persons think we are lovable so that they will love the selves we know ourselves not to be, in order that we might begin loving the persons they mistakenly think we are. This process spirals us into a self-disdain that makes us a burden to ourselves—even becoming sick over the lives we have been dealt and the selves we are forced to inhabit.

When such efforts at self-love come to their inevitable dead end, the problem that is exposed is not that we cannot love God if we cannot love ourselves. Rather, we cannot love ourselves unless we are first loved by God. John puts this clearly: "In this is love, not that we loved God but that he loved us and sent his Son to be the atoning sacrifice for our sins" (1 John 4:10). Unable to heal ourselves, we need to be healed. We need to get the heart of the gospel straight—that the love we so deeply need is initiated by God not because we are lovable but in spite of our being unlovable. William of Thierry distills the idea further. He writes to God, "You first loved us so that we might love you—not because you needed our love, but because we could not be what you created us to be, except by loving you."

What a crucial reversal. Thus only the unwarranted and unearned love of God in Christ can free us from this disease of self-centeredness. Then, in thankfulness for being so loved, we are open to love others as we are being loved—in turn becoming a bit lovable ourselves.

Being illustrative from my own life, early in my childhood I experienced anxiety about being abandoned. My solution was to become so worth keeping that I could guarantee not being thrown away. While this dynamic forged an outwardly responsible and hardworking person, it escalated into a workaholism that brought me to burnout. Inside I was a driven, lonely, and insecure competitor. The fatigue of unremitting doing exposes the heresy of self-help, for one is no longer able to keep filled the leaky tank of "worthiness."

But we need God's gift more than once. Only through the discipline of daily rehearsal are we able to counter our deep feelings of being unlovable. I temper this drive that had mastered me through a liturgy of repetition, posting on my bathroom mirror, front door, computer, and dashboard the scripture that affirms all I need to know and reknow. "Who will separate us from the love of Christ? . . . I am convinced that neither death, nor life, nor angels, nor rulers, nor things present, nor things to come, nor powers, nor height, nor depth, nor anything else in all creation, will be able to separate us from the love of God in Christ Jesus our Lord" (Rom. 8:35, 38-39). The childhood hymn has finally become my mantra: "Jesus loves me! This I know." Not surprisingly, my favorite hymn is God's promise to each of us: "Though all hell should endeavor to shake, I'll never, no, never, no, never forsake." God both creates and satisfies our primal longing.

➤ Create a mantra that expresses the promise you most need to be fulfilled in order to be whole.

Senses

ONE AT A TIME TOGETHER

Each of us has a favorite sense—one of the five that provides us with a secret passageway of receptivity into the sacred. The two mottoes hanging in the music alcove of my hermitage identify mine: "God gave us music that we might pray without words," and "Music, as the soul's deepest language, is the speech of God." Hearing is my favorite sense. The spiritual access for others might be sight—ranging from the lure of an unfolding sunrise to the gentle shading of a Renoir painting. For others, it is smell, with the fragrance of a flower able to coax the invisible into presence. For others, it is touch, as the tangible feel of another hand diffusing otherness into tenderness. For still others, there is ecstasy in the taste of wild strawberries with cream. We are blessed by poets who shape the words of our hearts, musicians who distinguish flowers by their songs, and woodworkers who thrill with the aroma of cedar.

In offering a course in worship, I once invited a ballet instructor to team-teach with me. Why not, for liturgy aches to be choreographed, its words a poetry shaped into gestures by the passion that induced David to dance naked before the Lord. During that semester, I began to sense how each of us not only has a master sense but also how our other senses form a hierarchical arrangement that forms a texture all its own. I remember experiencing this one spring evening when I was failing magnificently in trying to master this activity called contemplation. I finally gave up. And without warning, I heard the silence speak. I was sitting by an open window when everything stopped. Wrapped in the hushed sounds of stillness, a warm breeze fondled my face with a hint of pine branch music. Cattle in the valley lowed the grace notes, the evening snuggled in for sleep, and whip-poor-wills began cheering the moon in her levitation.

Contemplative silence is an invitation into this inexhaustible sensual beauty of attentive living—a child giggling for no clear reason, the soft touch of a kitten's purring, a goblet of wine reflected by a crackling fire, the harmonics of a Bach fugue as the world's invitation into dance. Life is not a course to be audited but an honors major to be chosen. "Praise the LORD! . . . sun and moon . . . shining stars . . . fire and hail, snow and frost . . . mountains and all hills, fruit trees and all cedars . . . creeping things and flying birds!" (Ps. 148:1-10). With senses teased into aliveness by the Holy Spirit, we can "taste and see that the LORD is good" (Ps. 34:8).

➤ **Arrange your five senses in the order of their power over you. Intentionally practice each as an instrument of praise.**

Silent Simplicity

AS SANITY

*T*rappist monasteries seem like strange places to outsiders. In making contemplation their reason for being, the Trappists are ascetics in sound and sight. Their ideal for centuries was total silence except for chanting, communicating only when absolutely necessary with sign language. Silence remains normative, but since Vatican II the wiser dictum is to "speak only when it improves the silence." Even so, this is done only in designated places so that the silence of others is not disturbed. The day begins and ends by being wrapped in the "Great Silence."

While some may regard such silence as excessive, our society has reached the point where the opposite is truly excessive. Around us and plugged into us are noisy busyness, incessant chattering, and competitive clatter. We feel naked without sound plugged into our ears, and we are constantly on edge expecting our cell phones to ring. Our fleeting thoughts are controlled by their translatability into Facebook entries. Companies put callers on hold so as to invade their captive ears with sales pitches. Elevator music cloaks the awkwardness of standing close to others without saying something.

Not only does noise accost our ears, but our eyes are bombarded with sights. Every surface, stationary or moving, is a potential advertising space. Repetition is incessant in bludgeoning our resistance. A hundred channels of TV huckstering reinforce our daily deluge of junk mail. In fact, all our senses are assaulted. Expensively acquired gourmet tastes groom us away from fresh garden simplicity. Canned fragrances compete with fresh air for marking special occasions.

With our minds and senses so pickpocketed by overload, the simplicity of silence is an endangered species. "You want to get away?" asks a television ad. Yes, indeed, but not on a flight to a more expensive version of the same. *Nervous breakdown* is the term for a desperate body forced to pull the plug on itself. Our less drastic coping mechanism is obliviousness, developing an inner mute button so that our hearing is not a listening, and our looking is not seeing. And while a faded bumper sticker suggests we "Take Time to Smell the Roses," the only available flowers are the fake ones at the mall.

Ascetic, abstemious, moderate, temperate—such words characterize the monastic lifestyle that takes seriously the prophets who insist that Divine judgment weighs heavy on those who choose excess. Ours is a society ruled by excess, and we can feel the edges of Divine reckoning. Global warming, polluted air, contaminated water, depletion of raw materials, nuclear waste, world hunger, vulgar opulence—these are the cannibalistic inscriptions of our upwardly mobile lifestyle destined to destroy the earth.

This big picture is bleak, but so is the smaller one. Stifling is the cost being extracted from each of us just by living in such a society. Whether or not our system can survive in the long haul, each of us in the short haul requires the sanity of periodic time away. Monasteries persevere as remnants proffering "forced feeding" to recapture a predilection for silence, a respect for the simple, a mindfulness of beauty, a purity of taste, and a yearning for an intentional living retrofitted as welcoming residences for the Holy Spirit. Such retreats must become regular if this alternative sensitivity is to become an acquired taste. Between times, I suggest as a hermitage a brown bag lunch in a cemetery, a nook in the public library, sea lions at the zoo, a neighborhood church, a special corner in any room, or one's car with Gregorian chant. Once the *what* is tasted, the *wheres* will follow generously.

Where do you go to gain a sanity fix? How frequently do you schedule visits?

Spirituality

AN EXERCISE IN ALTERNATION

Christian spirituality is different for each person, which is a good reason for spiritual direction. My seminary roommate left in the middle of our first year, and I hadn't a clue as to why. I understand now. I am an extrovert, loving people and places and activity of all kinds. In our Old Testament class, Moses became my instant hero—the liberator who freed his people, parted the Red Sea, and courageously led them toward the Promised Land.

But my roommate was an introvert. Not only did Moses-like extroverts leave him cold, but also seeing graphic extroversion throughout the Bible was his final reason for leaving. If only he would have stayed until we got to Elijah, for here is modeled an alternative understanding. We see a solitary Elijah at the mouth of a cave, unable to find God in the harsh external happenings of tornado, earthquake, and fire. Instead, he heard the God who spoke in a "still small voice" (1 Kings 19:12, KJV). Only later, as a professor, did I realize the connection between our diverse personalities and our contrasting understandings of God.

I was born an extrovert child of two introvert parents. Their God was the "still small voice." But attempts at imposing this spirituality on me only elicited mischievousness—making me feel that I hadn't a spiritual bone in my body. Seminary gave me permission to carve out an extroverted spirituality—recognizing God as incarnated in relationships and objects and games and galaxies and humor and tears and laughter. I was freed to live a spirituality of picking dandelions, feeding pigeons, rooting for the Kansas City Chiefs, and embracing Mickey Mouse as my patron saint.

Now, as a spiritual director, by discerning diverse personalities I can sense the God that each person is seeking and where he or she might best look to find the God who speaks his or her native tongue.

After we discover a spirituality that best fits his or her personality and arrange accountability for practicing it, the next step in growth is to walk into the *shadow*. This is the undeveloped dimensions of one's personality—the opposite of one's strengths. Jesus models this when after thirty years of introvert living, he is called into an extroverted charisma that holds crowds spellbound, healing and teaching to the point of exhaustion. Then he dismisses the crowds, needing to be fed again in the silence of the hills, sometimes praying all night. What Jesus models as ideal is a spirituality of alternation. The fullness of Christian personhood involves a disciplined pendulum swing between engagement and solitude, sensing and imagination, feeling and thinking, openness and commitment. We must learn to hear the still small voice even when bombarded by the noise, busyness, competitiveness, and violence of today's world. Once recharged with inner tranquillity, we might be able to dance on Main Street in the glory of God.

The church's worship according to the liturgical year supports us in living this spiritual pendulum; it invites us into the rhythms of high and low, singing and silence, fulfillment and longing, action and stillness, togetherness and aloneness. Epiphany's mission follows the deepness of Advent longings. Lenten sacrifices erupt into Pentecostal singing. Without Ash Wednesday and Good Friday fasts, Christmas and Easter feasts might seem over the top. Saint Bruno characterized the texture of this alternating spirituality as the rhythm of "leisure that is full and activity that is tranquil."

❧ **How does your personality affect your faith perspective? What would it be like to develop intentionally your shadow side?**

Taking for Granted

AS YUCKINESS

Sin is a yucky business, both in its consequences and in the attitude out of which it oozes. My candidate for sin's least common denominator is the attitude of taking things for granted. Life begins to go wrong when we find ourselves bored with it. Once this dynamic sets in, it takes on a life of its own, trivializing spring rains, flowers, full moons, friends, and even morning coffee. The sun comes up just to go back down; the wind blows from the north only to turn around from the south. Rain runs from rivers to the ocean only to evaporate and start the same tired process over again. "All things are wearisome . . . nothing new under the sun" (Eccles. 1:8-9).

The modern version? *Been there, done that.* The daily treadmill we find ourselves on strains under an overload of sameness. Watching the drained crowds on their way to work, T. S. Eliot—quoting Dante— sighed, "I had not known that death had undone so many."

This disposition may not sound very harmful when lived in small amounts, but these small doses can deposit a depressed dusting over everything—one's spouse, children, home, church, job, income, health, neighborhood, and self. But is it sinful? It can be. At its heart lurks the poisonous assumption that we deserve not only all we have but more. *Entitlement* is a good term for it, assuming that the world owes us. The result is arrogance, haughtiness, self-importance, and condescension. When life is no longer a big deal, neither are persons or things that may get in the way. When more and more feels like less and less, what difference does it make?

Psychologically this state is called *narcissism* or self-obsession. Theologically it is called *pride*, the arrogance of acting as a god. In everyday experience, this pride is the nastiness of persons acting as if they know it all and notifying others as to how they should live their lives. This yuckiness is easy to perceive in others; in our own selves, however, it can be difficult to spot.

With scripture as our medical manual, step one in curing nastiness is the medicine of an awakening. This awakening comes in assorted shapes and sizes. Anything will do if it is sufficient to puncture our feigned superiority. Disappointment, failure, defeat—each can be an opportunity for rebirth. These moments of deflation can push us toward being teachable. With the threat of having our lives and everything we care for swept away, we can be awakened to the preciousness of what we have. To be born again is to be refitted with a childlike disposition to savor fully each day. Here is resurrection, evoked through intense regret over the possibility of loss. It is in experiencing things as if for the last time that there can be reborn the miracle of experiencing them again as if for the first time. Such an awakening rekindles a sense of awe. The longing to taste, hear, see, smell, be touched if only one more time. It is said that we look at the world once, in childhood; the rest is memory. Not so for those reborn into childlikeness.

We might call this *Edenic seeing*—as when God looked over creation and saw that it was good. This remembrance has the power to purge boredom and insert a deep thankfulness. "Morning Has Broken" is the hymn of choice, with each dawn fresh like the first day in a re-creation of what "Eden saw play!" Blackbirds, spring rain, dew, sunlight—all of it now, still.

➵ **What aspects of your living will you most miss at death? How are you forfeiting them already?**

Why Is This So Difficult?

WHEN IT ISN'T

I still remember the punch line of a TV commercial from long ago. After the actor shows off the amazing qualities of a product that I don't remember, he looks up incredulously and asks, "Why is this so difficult?" We Christians have a penchant for making the simplicity of our faith downright complex. We desire to have spelled out in detail what we are to do, when, toward whom, how often, and when we can stop. For Jesus, rules are simply illustrations of how to live a faith that is not itself governed by rules.

This is why Jesus taught primarily through storytelling. While he drew from multiple situations, his parables all have one simple plot, told in various ways so that at least through one story that plot can become ours. It is why each of us probably has a favorite parable, one that is our story of stories.

My favorite story concerns a tiny, black lamb. The other sheep ostracize her for being different, and in feeling unwanted, she comes to believe that she is not worth being wanted. If she is dumb and unlovable, then it hardly matters what she does. Whether thoughtful or mischievous, she will never belong. This heaviness descends over her until there comes a day when she just doesn't care anymore—so she lets herself wander off. The farther she drifts away, the more certain she is that if the other sheep do notice, it will be with a snicker of, "Good riddance." Night comes, and the darkness is darker than she recalls it ever being before. She hears strange noises. She is cold, hungry, and frightened. It's all over, and she knows it.

Yet, sometime during that shivering night, she dares to think she hears within the harsh wind a hint of a familiar voice, even the sound of her name. She had been anxious, but now it is guilt and panic that chokes her. It is the shepherd. He had to leave all his ninety-nine sheep just because of her. She fears she is within seconds of a sound thrashing or worse. But there are neither angry words nor a blow from his staff. Instead, he lifts her gently, wraps her in his own cloak, and after a long embrace puts her securely on his shoulders, saying, "I've missed you!" The shepherd himself understands what it means to be scorned and abused. And so home they go, laughing all the way. Why is this so difficult?

➤ **Which biblical parable most qualifies as your story of stories? Why?**

Work

MEANS AS ENDS?

One of the most heartrending scriptural portraits is Moses on his final afternoon. He remembers how God plucked him from a shepherd's life and forced him against his will on an absurd mission to demand that the mighty Pharaoh liberate his highly profitable slaves. Then he was told to care for God's people in an utterly inhospitable desert for forty years. God finally gives him the green light to bring his people to the Promised Land. Near the boundary, God leads Moses to the summit of Mount Nebo, there feasting his eyes upon the goal. Then comes God's stinging declaration: "I have let you see it with your eyes, but you shall not cross over there" (Deut. 34:4). The saddest of tears may be shed by those who can see their promise only from afar.

Such scriptural pathos is not rare. David, for example, yearned to climax his faithful life by building a magnificent temple for God but was told that his son would be the one to do it. Then there is Jesus, who during his final week looks out upon his beloved Jerusalem and sobs, "How often have I desired to gather your children together as a hen gathers her brood under her wings, and you were not willing!" (Luke 13:34). Each of our lives will end with some sad version of never seeing the harvesting of seeds we sowed. No matter how long our lives, death will always feel premature.

In facing this inevitability, I find helpful the way work is approached at the monastery. Each morning the bulletin board announces our daily assignment. Work begins with bells, ends with bells, and bells season our work with worship. Absorbed in our assigned projects, often the ringing is a surprise. Yet we stop, immediately. A thrust of the brush into thinner, a quick wash of hands, a robe flipped over one's blue jeans, and off we go to church. In the quiet chanting our unfinished work is offered as gift. What remains undone will patiently wait until I—or someone else—am chosen to pick up where I left off.

What a contrast such living is to our accomplishment-driven American living, gauging meaning by how many things we can scratch off the list. Even on day's off, the myth is that by working hard enough we can salvage some time just to be. Yet lists are self-generating, guaranteeing that we will never reach the end. Measuring meaning by the quantity of completions drains the qualitative joy of doing, hurried by the more always waiting to be done.

So it was with Israel, for only after their dream began turning sour in the land flowing with milk and honey did they realize that what made the desert years difficult was their impatience to reach the goal. Yet those years were really their honeymoon with God. God had wooed Israel to be a wedded beloved, tasting together the joy of companionship, needing little more than a daily allotment of manna. But in reaching their goal, they forfeited the means by which they had arrived. Many a divorce begins when in attaining the split-level dream, the couple forget their first years in a small, one-bedroom apartment when all that mattered was that they had each other.

In authentic Christian living, the journey is equally as important as the arrival, the making as joyous as the completing, the quality of the doing as precious as the beauty of the "done." When accomplishing and accomplished commingle, getting the dishwashing done is spiced by playfulness amid the soapsuds. Whatever cannot be done with joy in the doing should make us wonder if it is worth doing at all. I would like to believe that on his last afternoon, Moses picked blackberries to share with God.

➶ How does your being (or not being) a list-maker serve you positively? negatively?

Worship

THE BIG PICTURE

Although worship is key to being a Christian, many of us are confused about what it's all about. The clue for me came in realizing that authentic worship is rooted in its structure. We find in Isaiah's moving encounter with God in the temple a model for how the church has shaped not only prayer but also worship. His experience is structured by a fourfold sequence: *adoration* ("Holy, holy, holy"); *confession* ("Woe is me!"); *affirmation* ("your guilt has departed"); and *dedication* ("Here am I; send me!") (Isa. 6:3-8). This personal progression, in turn, identifies the basic structure of God's drama that gives history its plot. Together, *adoration, confession, affirmation,* and *dedication* shape our Sunday worship as the personal experience of being drawn into an hour pilgrimage—from creation's beginning, through rebellion and forgiveness, into a feeding as foretaste, and then sent out as colaborers in kingdom building.

Let's see how this works. The prelude sets the atmosphere of mystery, of expectant waiting, as when the Spirit first moved over the face of the void, birthing light from darkness and time from stillness. The first act begins as we rise with a hymn of adoration in awe of God's majestic act of creation, as when on the first morning the stars danced for joy. *Eden* is its name, and God births us as Adams and Eves singing "Holy, holy, holy," amazed that we are called forth as cocreators into creation.

Confession, as the second act, is a retelling of the whispered temptation our ancestors heard—eat of this tree, and you will be as God. We continue to participate in the Fall—as we recall our arrogance in clutching the world to ourselves, playing god by doing whatever we want, whenever we want, to anyone who gets in our way of getting what we want. Adam and Eve and we concoct fig-leaf disguises to hide the naked silliness of our petty god-playing games. "Where are you?" comes a voice in the cool of the evening, under a canopy of endlessly dancing galaxies. And suddenly our trifling lives appear paltry—unclean. Confession is our acknowledgment of participating in this arrogant sub-plot that keeps playing itself out throughout history. Only the names of the actors change—Adam/Eve; Cain/Abel; you/me. The confession begins as we, then in concreteness as me. Waiting, in the deep silence, are incredible words of forgiveness: "Though your sins are like scarlet, they shall be like snow" (Isa. 1:18). With a sprinkling recalling our baptismal cleansing, we break forth in a grateful singing of the Gloria or some other psalm of thanksgiving.

Cleansed of heart, we enter act three to explore the fuller context of affirmation. The Hebrew scriptures provide variations on the theme of promise, followed by the gospel as its fulfillment. The power of this pronouncement is visually reinforced sometimes when an adorned Bible is processed to the lectern in a recalling of Jesus' Palm Sunday arrival. Some congregations sign their foreheads, lips, and hearts, asking for an open mind, a responding tongue, and a believing soul. Then all is ready as we rise in recognition of Christ's real presence in scripture as the Word within the words. After a sermonic appropriation and a creedal promise of obedience, prayers of intercession begin the translation of hearing into action in and for the world.

Since most early Christians were Jews, these acts thus far reflect the flow of synagogue worship that they knew—adoration, confession, forgiveness, scriptural affirmation, explication, and intercessions. But in addition, they participated in the sacrificial worship of the temple. Thus the climax of act three occurs when they enter the upper room of their new temple. Here occurs the play within the play—the center point of history and of our worship. During Holy Communion, the broken bread and poured-out wine become the Divine-human sacrifice in a Golgotha that is ongoing. The eucharistic prayer is that the resurrected Christ known at Emmaus will be reexperienced here as a real presence in the breaking of bread. The Communion of our eating and drinking is our participation in the Easter breakfast on a Galilean seashore—with Christ's resurrection continuing as he becomes incarnate in us.

Dedication, as the fourth act, is our response to all that God has done. The Catholic word for worship is *mass*, from the Latin root of the word *dismissal*, meaning "to be sent out." Worship is our dress rehearsal for being dismissed out into the world to become Eucharist and to live as prayer, having rehearsed the promised vision of a new heaven and a new earth. "Go therefore and make disciples of all nations" (Matt. 28:19). The final benediction is a mini-Pentecost, empowered by the Holy Spirit "to go in peace to love and serve our God and one another." Thus worship is an experiential immersion in the sweep of history, from inception to promised consummation, in which the plot of our own small lives is taken up into the sweeping choreography of God.

⤳ **How might understanding worship as drama enrich your own experience? the experience of your local church?**